D0878195

No Sweat Pants
Allowed
- Wine Club

Jan Romes

FROM

Cover Design: Tugboat Design
Formatting: Tugboat Design
www.tugboatdesign.net

No Sweat Pants Allowed – Wine Club
Copyright 2015 Janice Romes
All Rights Reserved

This book is licensed for your personal enjoyment only. This book may not be resold or given away to other people. If you would like to share this book with another person, please purchase an additional copy for each recipient. If you're reading this book and did not purchase it, or if it not purchased for your use only then please purchase your own copy. Thank you for respecting the hard work of this author.

This is a work of fiction. Names, characters, places and incidents are either the product of the author's imagination or are used fictitiously, and any resemblance to actual persons, living or dead, events, or locales is entirely coincidental.

To Bill, always!

Big love to:
BJ, Kerri, Elyse, Malia, Valarie, and Liam
Kelly, Sam, and Jax

A special dedication to the members of the Monday
Night Therapy gang who are a unique joy!

To Betsy R. - Thank you for your insight when I
bounced my idea off you for Grace's character. You
helped me understand it was okay the way I wanted to
handle her situation. I'm deeply grateful!

Dear Readers,

As many of you know, my genre is romance. I've decided to also take the plunge into women's fiction with this book. This story has been bouncing through my thoughts for a long time and I decided it was time to breathe life into the characters who were begging for attention.

No Sweat Pants Allowed – Wine Club is Elaina Samuels's story but it couldn't happen without Tawny Westerfield, Stephanie Mathews and Grace Cordray.

Life has given them lemons, but the lemonade they make is darn tasty. Their journeys to get life right-side-up are hilarious and heartrending, sarcastic and sassy. They deliver mayhem and mischief, and a few powerful messages, too.

I'd be remiss if I didn't mention, Stony, the adorable Siberian Husky who tries to steal the show on more than one occasion.

Let the fun begin!

Love,
Jan

'The greatest healing therapy is friendship and love.'

~ Hubert H. Humphrey

No
Sweat Pants
Allowed

- Wine Club

Chapter One

~ *Monkeys Unite* ~

Sandwiched between two very large guys – one who smelled like he'd eaten a dozen cloves of garlic, the other who must've bathed in beer – Elaina Samuels, checked her watch, shifted from foot to foot, and finally inhaled; not because she wanted to, but a girl could only hold her breath for so long before turning blue and passing out.

Leaning around the wide back of garlic-man to hawk-eye the front of the line, Elaina grumbled under her breath, "Come on, people. How long does it take to get rid of your unwanted gold?"

Garlic-man did a half-turn. "I know, right?" His gaze roamed over her, sending a cold shiver up Elaina's spine. Lingering at her chest for an inordinately long moment, he moved up to meet her eyes with a salacious smile and a large chunk of broccoli wedged between his front teeth.

It wasn't a whole spear, but it stuck out like one.

Elaina fought the urge to point to the funky green stuff. Instead, she squinted with reproach.

The smelly man appeared unaffected by her glare.

"Who's doing all the whimpering?"

Elaina had also heard the woeful sounds. Slightly nauseous from the combination of scents assaulting her airspace, with her last nerve hanging by a fragile thread, she replied blandly, "I have no idea." If the pungent doofus didn't face forward, he'd soon be plucking poison darts from his forehead; not that she had any darts, but if she did he'd be in a world of hurt.

The husky man behind, slurred his two cents about the weepy woman in the back of the store. "What's her deal? If she didn't want to part with her jewelry, why come here?"

Elaina was torn between telling them both to mind their own beeswax and actually finding some darts to impale their foreheads. "What are you guys, the jewelry police?"

"Funny." Garlic-man inched closer.

The whiny guy who had the essence of a brewery rolling off him, snorted with impatience. "I'm not waiting any longer." He hollered to the jeweler. "Your ad is false, buddy. It said quick appraisals and easy transactions. I've been waiting for forty-five minutes and the line hasn't moved. I can find better ways to waste my time," he spat – literally.

Elaina shuddered when droplets hit her cheek.

The disturbing sounds coming from the back of the room continued, making her even more anxious. She toyed with the 18 karat gold wedding band she'd slid from her left hand to her right five days ago.

Garlic-man cocked an eyebrow. "So what's *your* deal?"

He eyed the ring.

The fine blonde hairs on Elaina's arms stood up like she was about to be struck by lightning. Lowering her hand to keep him from staring, she imagined one of those poison darts piercing his cranium. An acerbic reply made its way to the tip of her tongue.

As a business woman it would behoove her to let it go. As a woman whose heart and temperament were a mess from last week's court appearance, she couldn't hold back. Her eyes jetted to his mammoth pot belly. "I own a gym, so my *deal* is fitness." It took all her willpower not to add, "If you'd like to work off all those donuts let me know." She winced inwardly at the meanness rolling around in her thoughts. It wasn't like her to put anyone down. If anything, she propped people up with positive reinforcement. Elaina swallowed hard. Last week her marriage officially ended. At the same time, her tolerance for asshats must've crumbled too. Tempted to tell the guy he needed a mint, she stepped from the line. "Sorry. I didn't mean to take my bad mood out on you." Before he could call her a name that rhymed with itch, she headed for the exit.

Reaching the revolving doors, she identified the person making the soulful sounds. A short-haired woman dressed completely in black held a clump of used tissues.

Something Elaina had seen on Facebook shadowed her thoughts: Not my circus, not my monkeys. She'd laughed at the time. Now she considered adopting it as her motto. The only way to get a fresh start was to forget the chaos of the last few years and not get trapped in someone else's. She heaved a heavy breath and pushed through the door.

Donning sunglasses against the brilliant June sun, Elaina shoved the strap of her purse higher on her shoulder, and was set to take the paver-brick walkway to the public parking lot in the rear of the building. She made the mistake of looking through the jewelry store window. The weepy woman's head was downcast and Elaina's heart clenched. She might have her own issues to work through, but she couldn't knowingly walk away from someone in distress.

She turned on her heel and trekked back inside to the woman with jet black hair, a pasty white complexion, and light blue eyes thickly lined with black eyeliner. The weeper was strikingly beautiful in a Goth-like way. "Are you okay?"

Watery eyes connected with Elaina's. "I'm a wreck."

Crap. Elaina had hoped for a different response; like 'I'm fine' or 'It's my allergies'. "Care to talk about it?" *Please say no.*

"I can't do this, yet I have to," the woman sniveled.

Now what?

"Ohhh, thank goodness," came a soft voice beside them. "I wanted to offer comfort but I was afraid I'd be told to butt out."

Elaina surveyed the buttinski whose red hair was pulled up in a trendy-messy bun and automatically did a fitness assessment – a hazard of the job. She snickered inwardly, wondering if it was actually a fitness thing or the instinctive nature of being female kicking in; one woman appraising another. The buttinski was rather meaty, yet attractive. Clad in an Ohio State t-shirt and grey sweat pants cut off just below the knees, she'd finished the casual look with red flip flops. Each ear sparkled with three diamond post earrings. "I'm sure…" Elaina gestured to the Goth-ish woman.

Blotting the corners of her eyes with a tissue, the woman sniffed. "Grace."

Elaina continued. "I'm sure Grace won't pierce our cranium with a poison dart for butting in."

Grace and Red looked confused by the comment and simultaneously said, "Huh?"

The remark had been silly. Trying to explain it would be even sillier. "Never mind."

Something bumped Elaina's arm. Reflexes made her draw back. When she realized it was a pair of torpedo boobs that smacked into her, she started to laugh but stopped abruptly and issued a small frown to the owner of those puppies. "Excuse me?"

Torpedo-boobs' dark-brown eyes gleamed with amusement. "They get ahead of me sometimes."

The four women broke into a laugh.

Elaina extended her hand. "Elaina Samuels."

Torpedo boobs introduced herself at Tawny Westerfield.

Grace quietly said, "Grace Cordray."

Lastly, Red spoke up. "I'm Stephanie Mathews, but I prefer Steph."

"It's nice to meet you Grace, Stephanie, and Tawny." Elaina looked around the crowded jewelry store. "This isn't a good place to talk. There's a bar across the street. Anyone in the mood for a mid-afternoon glass of fermented grapes?"

"A thousand times yes." Grace was through the revolving door before Tawny and Steph had a chance to answer.

Steph shrugged. "She clearly needs to vent. I wouldn't mind doing the same thing."

"Nothing like alcohol to loosen the tongue." Tawny smirked. "I'm in."

Again, Elaina's inner-critic warned, Not my circus; not my monkeys. Yeah, well, she was going to bypass the voice of reason and buy three monkeys a glass of wine.

* * *

"Give us minute." Elaina smiled up at the spiky-haired bartender.

The thirty-something guy whose muscles stretched the fabric of his Under Armor shirt in all the right places, ignored Elaina and winked at Tawny. "Take your time, ladies. When you're ready to order give me a wave." He walked away with a cocky swagger.

Tawny fanned herself with the leather-bound wine list. "If I was ten years younger…" She scrunched her face into a mess of tight lines. "Listen to me. The ink is barely dry on the divorce papers and I'm panting after the first guy who looked at my boobs." She shoved her fingers into the breast pocket of her leopard print shirt and retrieved a set of white-gold wedding rings. Holding them up so the light hit the diamonds, she let out a mirthless laugh and dropped them onto the varnished wood table. The clinking sound perked up a couple at a nearby table. They turned to check out the noise. "My bad." Tawny scooped up the rings and haphazardly threw them into her purse. "We're here to console Grace."

Grace patted Tawny's arm. "We're not here for just me."

Steph picked at her fingernails. "I think we all have a story to tell."

Elaina sifted air through her teeth. Airing dirty laundry to complete strangers might not be a good idea. After all, Cherry Ridge, Ohio was a decent size city but gossip seemed to make its way around as if it was a small town. She raised her cheeks in an impish grin. "I'm here to get soused."

"You might've suggested this adventure but I doubt it was to get toasted. Steph's right. You have something to get off your chest too," Tawny quipped.

"Oh I'm going to get toasted." Elaina tried to discount Steph and Tawny's pinpoint accuracy with a casual chuckle.

Tawny continued to dig. "Is it something you do regularly?"

"Almost never," rushed out of Elaina's mouth in subconscious defense. The pressure of three sets of eyes bearing down on her made the truth surface. "My ex made sure I behaved at all times. He was a killjoy with a capital K. So no, getting toasted isn't something I do regularly."

Tawny nudged Steph with her forearm. "She does have a story. Let's see, I have an ex and so does Elaina. How about you, Steph? Grace?"

Steph curled her upper lip in a sneer. "I have an ex all right; an ex-fiancé. A week before the wedding, the jackal decided he wanted a tall, leggy blonde whose 36D-cups runneth over, instead of a chunky redhead who's lucky to be a 34A." A long, cavernous sigh rolled out. "I also have an ex-husband from a mistake I made right out of high school. But that's ancient history. We were clueless kids who wanted to play house. A month in, we wanted to un-play house. He was a good guy. It was just the wrong time. Technically, I have two exes but only one I want to run over with a bus."

"A week before? What a bastard!" Elaina shifted in the booth. She was a champion for the underdog. The trait was one of many things that drove her now-ex-husband, Arden, up a wall. According to him, people needed to deal with their own troubles without her offering a shoulder. Translation: he had no capacity for compassion and he wanted her undivided attention.

"Bastard," Steph repeated as though trying to determine if the name fit the man who'd broken her heart.

Grace closed her eyes. "I'm a widow," she said softly.

Elaina offered a sympathetic, "Aww." Tawny and Steph mimicked the response.

Grace's eyelashes fluttered with tears edging the corners of her eyes. "It's still too new."

"How long has it been?" Tawny ventured.

"Two years."

Elaina, Tawny, and Steph exchanged surprised looks.

Having lost both parents early in life, Elaina knew the power of grief. It was as strong as a barnacle on the bottom of a boat; dragging you down and sucking your strength. You can scrape it. Power-wash it. Hit it with a rubber mallet. Realistically, it takes a jackhammer of caring people to get the sucker to let go. In her case, it had been friends, neighbors, cousins, and her employees at the gym who'd offered comfort, not her husband. Sadly, due to Arden's stringent, unfeeling personality, one by one her close friends wandered away until she had zero.

Elaina pulled Grace into a fierce hug. "I'm here for you, chick." It was a weird thing to say to someone newly met, but deep inside it felt right. "I'm here for all of you."

"Wow. We're a pitiful foursome." Tawny chewed on her thumbnail. "Two divorcees, one dumpee, and a Gothee-widow."

Elaina was glad Tawny lightened the moment.

Grace swiped at the briny rivulets continuing to stream from her eyes. "I'm not Goth." She sniffed and displayed a hand with a type of French tip polish. Instead of clear polish with white tips, hers were lacquered in black and tipped in grey. "I'm more ghoulish than Goth-ish."

"You're still in mourning," Steph said.

"I guess so." Grace huffed out a breath. "I'm tired of the grief. Although, all the bawl-babying I did at the jewelry store and just now, one would think otherwise." She ran her fingers gently over her wedding rings. "I don't see how I can part with these. But if I don't, I'll never be able to move on." She sat up straighter. "I need to hear your stories so I can forget mine for a while. Tell us more, Elaina."

"Not without a drink." Elaina motioned to the handsome flirt who'd returned from the back room carrying a case of Bud Light long necks.

In a flash, he was there. "Have you lovely ladies decided?"

Elaina ordered first. "I'll try a bottle of blackberry wine." She read the description from the wine list. "The blackberry aromas will prepare your senses for a gentle, modestly sweet treat. Oh yeah. That's what I'm talking about."

Mr. Tight-jeans Flat-abs raised a sexy eyebrow. "A bottle and four glasses?"

"Sure."

Tawny spoke to the bartender in a sultry voice. "Also bring us a bottle of dry red." Looking at the wine list, she rattled off, "It full-bodied, yet approachable, with a forward balance of black cherries and oak."

His blue eyes sparkled as if she'd come on to him. "Definitely full-bodied." The remark was as noticeably suggestive as Tawny's.

Steph rolled her eyes but her mouth split into a smile. "I'm going for the luscious, zesty Sangria." She ran her tongue slowly and exaggeratedly over her lips. To mock Tawny? Or an attempt to win the hunk's attention?

Elaina shook with restrained laughter.

Grace smiled sweetly. "Would you like to buy some

wedding rings?"

The blond dude appeared dazed.

"Oops. I mean, I'll try a bottle of white Merlot." Grace nipped at her bottom lip.

"A bottle of gentle and modestly sweet for you." He pointed to Elaina. "Full-bodied and approachable for…"

Tawny cut in. "Tawny."

"For Tawny." His gaze skimmed across her phenomenal chest.

Steph didn't miss a beat. "Hey!" She jerked her thumb up as though she was trying to get him to look away from Tawny's chest.

The well-built, taking-it-all-in stud struck back with a gravelly snicker. "Luscious and zesty for the redhead and white Merlot for the doll who wants to sell her wedding rings. Got it." He turned to fill their order, but swung back around. "You gorgeous vixens are going to get hammered, aren't you?"

Elaina fist-bumped Grace, then Tawny and Steph. "We're vixens."

The bartender chuckled his way back to the bar; possibly thinking, *Sweet. I'm going to have to put up with four drunken women.*

Elaina made a mental note to tip big.

* * *

Steph ran a finger around the rim of her glass. "We've taken the edge off with some wine. It's time to get down to the nitty-gritty of why we're here. Elaina, you were on a roll before we ordered."

Elaina splashed more wine into her glass and wet her lips with a taste. "I'm a health nut who owns a fitness center and exercises excessively." She beamed a smile and flexed her biceps, proud that she'd stayed in shape. "I was married to a man who was the biggest control freak on the planet." She paused to squelch an unexpected surge of emotion. "The Arden I married was a great guy...until he made his first million. Money slowly corrupted his head and his heart. He turned into a tyrant who took joy in micromanaging me." She tried to stop a growl but it came anyway. "I'm a grown woman who doesn't need someone telling me what I can and can't do." Another growl, louder than the first surprised Elaina, but she'd opened the tap and the anger was flowing. "If I had to pee I needed to clear it with him first."

"Seriously?" Grace asked.

"The bit about peeing isn't true, but you get the idea."

Steph's pencil-thin eyebrows bumped together. "Wait a minute." She snapped her fingers. "Arden Samuels? Of Samuels Accounting and Investment Firm? The guy's not only a multi-millionaire, he's also model material." A pink glow hit Steph's cheeks and she tried to backtrack. "Don't ask me where I heard it because I honestly don't remember."

"Arden Wellby Samuels has more money than he knows what to do with. He's a walking, talking bastard of a cliché – tall, dark, and ruthlessly handsome."

"Wellby? What's that all about?" Tawny's laugh was noticeably hoarse.

"I like you, Westerfield. You found the one thing about Arden that isn't attractive."

They high-fived.

The idea of millions hooked Steph. "Arden Wellby Samuels is loaded; which means, so are you."

Elaina grabbed the bottle of blackberry wine. Instead of refilling her glass, she drank straight from the bottle. "In exchange for his freedom, the barracuda was ordered to give me a one-time alimony payment, my SUV, the fitness center, and the house. Technically, I have money. Big whoop. The one thing I wanted from Arden, he wouldn't even consider. I wanted kids. One night in the middle of dinner, he tossed his napkin on his plate, and said, 'We're a mismatch. It's over.'" She drummed the table with her thumbs. "At forty-three I find myself alone, with baby-making parts that have never been used and no clear schematics for starting over."

Tawny messed with her phone and a mischievous grin slipped into her expression. She read what she'd found on Google. "Barracudas are voracious, opportunistic predators with large pointed heads. They rely on surprise and small bursts of speed to overtake their prey. Sound like your guy?"

Elaina bobbed her head up and down. "That's definitely him." Again, she tipped the bottle and took a healthy swallow. "Tawny, unravel your story. If you don't I may kill this whole bottle to deal with mine."

Tawny chewed her nails again; not that there were nails to chew. It looked like they'd been previously gnawed away. "I'm forty-six." She threw up a hand. "I know. How can I be forty-six and look this good?" She playfully wrinkled her nose. "I'm from hearty stock; equal parts Italian, Native American, Scotch-Irish, and Ohioan."

Elaina snorted. "How does Ohio fit into your lineage?"

"I threw it in to see if you were paying attention."

"You crack me up," Steph said.

Tawny tucked her shoulder-length hair behind her ears. "I like to clown around." The smile fell from her face. "But the truth is I'm an insecure piece of work." She laid her hand on the table to show her fingernails. "I'm a nurse who knows it's not healthy to chew your nails or smoke cigarettes. I do both." She paused as though waiting for them to condemn her. When they didn't, she continued. "I'm more of a closet smoker. When life gets the best of me, I light up." A genuine smile replaced her self-deprecation. "I'm also the proud mom of two sons. Bo lives in California and Quentin in Oregon." She shrugged. "Unlike Elaina, I'm barely scraping by."

Steph propped her elbows on the table. "Why are you an insecure piece of work?"

Tawny tapped the side of her glass. "I could blame overly-critical parents, but that's so cheesy. They're good people and I love them dearly. They just have a knack for nitpicking *every little thing*. Of course I fell for Grady Westerfield, who's a lot like them. Isn't that the way of it? Some women are drawn to the personality quirks they despise the most. Apparently I'm one of them." She lifted her shoulders in a second shrug. "I'm an imperfect woman who was trapped in a circle of perfectionists. I finally had enough and walked away. Grady convinced the judge he was getting the short end of the stick. As a result, the whiny skunk got the house, the camper, most of our savings, and the dog. I was lucky to get fifty thousand dollars, which had to be rolled into an IRA or Uncle Sam would've gotten a sizeable chunk. I still have my clunker of a car, which I affectionately call Ferdinand. Don't ask me why. I just do. Today, I was going to give my checkbook a boost by selling my rings. Sad state of affairs, right?"

"How does a skunk get custody of a dog?" Elaina asked humorously, but in no way was she trying to downplay that Tawny had gotten screwed twice; first by the skunk and then by the courts. When her comic relief fell flat, she reached across the table and squeezed Tawny's hand. "You're not insecure. If you were, you wouldn't be here."

Tawny bounced with a small laugh. "Grady's a fussy skunk. When he gets his fill of scooping up dog treasures and taking Stony out in the middle of the night to pee, he'll beg me to take the loveable pooch."

"Stony? Cool name." Grace brimmed with interest. "What kind of dog?"

"Siberian Husky."

"I love Huskies. They're big and shed like crazy but they're awesome. It's so cute when they lay on their backs with their feet in the air."

Tawny looked like she could cry. "When my kids moved away, Stony kept me from going off the deep end." She pushed out an exhale. "Even if Grady decides Stony is a pain, I can't take him. The apartment I moved into won't allow pets." She mimicked Elaina's move and drank straight from the bottle of dry red. She motioned to Steph. "I need to stop talking and you need to share more."

Steph folded her drink napkin into an accordion and fanned it over her face. "I'm forty, and like Elaina, childless. I have a tipped uterus and an insane proclivity for food. I'm a sap for men who walk all over me," she stated matter-of-factly. "When I'm happy, I eat. When I'm stressed, I eat. It doesn't help that I work as an executive assistant to a guy who goes a hundred miles an hour. Every day he taxes my self-control. I want to trip him to slow him down so I can catch up." She squinted. "And then there's Corbett, the good-for-nothing snake who discarded me like a worn out shoe. The slithering reptile broke up with me by text message. To cope, I made a mad dash to a carton of Cherry Garcia, moved on to a bag of fun-size Snickers, drank a case of Coke, and treated myself to a plate of cheese blintzes. Not all in one day, but I packed on twenty pounds." She tucked a wayward wisp of hair back into the bun. "He's not the reason I find myself in sweat pants, but he's a big part of my wretched reality. When things go extremely well or horribly awry, I go up a pant-size. If I don't stop eating or go shopping for new clothes soon," she tugged at the grey material, "I'll be wearing these blasted things to the office."

Grace looked stunned. "He broke up with you by text message?"

Steph's green eyes watered. "Sometimes technology sucks."

"Technology doesn't suck. The guy with no balls is what sucks. Big time."

"Amen to that." Steph fished a tissue from her purse to blow her nose.

Grace steepled her hands over her nose and mouth. "Even widowed at forty-one, I guess I'm lucky. My man was decent to me. Brince was a numbers cruncher for an insulation company. He was occasionally romantic and loved to cook. We have a son, Cody, who went to college for one year and dropped out to backpack around the world. He's currently in Italy, working as a waiter. Brince and I were at a good place in our lives. Our mortgage was paid. We had a little money in the bank and we were empty-nesters. One morning he got out of bed and keeled over." Her voice splintered and the tears returned. "The autopsy revealed a blockage in his main artery. They called it a widow maker."

"This may sound insensitive, Grace, but why were you going to get rid of your rings?"

Steph's lack of couth made Elaina frown.

"It's complicated. I loved Brince – and I always will – but I'm too young to be alone. Cody has said as much. We had a long talk last weekend when he called from Rome. He told me his dad would want me to find someone. I cried. He cried. I vowed to think about it. This morning I decided to go to the cash for gold event. I was going to trade in my rings and give the money to one of Brince's favorite charities. The second I stepped into the jewelry store my heart seemed to break all over again."

Elaina, Tawny, and Steph pulled Grace from the

booth and into a group hug.

"The four musketeers," Steph said.

"Yep," Elaina agreed, but she almost said four monkeys instead of musketeers.

Tawny wrenched them closer. "I hope we become inseparable friends."

Elaina's gaze slipped over Grace's shoulder in time to see the bartender approach. He quickly did an about-face like he was scared shitless of four emotional women. *The big chicken.*

"I don't want to cry anymore. I want to drink." Grace wiggled from the embrace and returned to the booth.

Tawny mentioned ordering food or they really would get toasted.

Elaina motioned for the handsome chicken with her finger.

"More wine, ladies?"

Grace drained her glass. "We definitely need more wine and food to soak it up."

"Excellent. I'll be right back with menus."

Steph poured the last of the Sangria into her glass, took a slow sip, and sat it down with a clunk. "Hide me!"

Elaina bunched her face in confusion. "Huh?"

Slinking down so her head was the only thing visible, the table muffled most of what Steph said. "Corbett and 36D's walked in." She cussed and tried to dip lower but there were too many legs in the way. "Of all the places he could go in this town, why here?"

Elaina stretched to glimpse the cad who'd used his phone to call things off. "Don't panic, sweetie, but they're headed this way."

Steph used the f-bomb freely but quietly.

Elaina sneered, sizing up Corbett as he approached. He wasn't good looking by most standards, but being homely wasn't a crime. Being homely and dumping someone as sweet and kind as Steph, however, should be a felony. She wondered what Corbett could've possibly exhibited to trick Steph's medial prefrontal cortex into thinking he was a good catch.

"Steph?" A wicked smile opened Corbett's dry, cracked lips. "Why are you wedged under the table?"

Elaina continued to turn her nose up at the stick-thin man with mousy brown hair. She appraised 36D's. The woman plastered to Corbett's side was blonde to the nth degree. Her hair was more bottle-white than bottle-blonde. To her benefit, she was taking everything in but saying nothing. Every few seconds, she snapped her gum.

"Dang. I can't find the cork." Steph drew up from under the table. "Ohhhh. Corbett."

Corbett-the-snake looked suspicious. "It's beside your bottle." His rough, gravelly voice made Elaina pucker with revulsion. He looked from woman to woman and settled his eyes on Tawny for too long.

Tawny gave him a slit-eyed look of loathing. "Boa constrictor or python?"

"You want me to pick one?"

"Noooo, I don't want you to pick one," Tawny spouted.

"Sleazy garden snake," Grace mumbled.

Corbett must've figured out they were referring

to him. His chest rose with forced laughter. "You gals helping Steph throw a pity party?"

Foul.

Elaina reared up, ready to give him an earful.

Steph stayed Elaina with her hand. Instead of ripping into him like she had every right to, she lifted her chin and smiled wickedly. "This is a wine club, jackass."

Corbett dropped his arm from the busty woman to put up his palms. "I'm not here to cause trouble so there's no need to get pissy."

Steph's shoulders drooped.

It was time to strike a match and burn his ass. "Pissy? You broke up with her by text message and she's not allowed to get pissy?" With each word Elaina got louder. "A real man would've had the decency to tell her in person." She grabbed the empty wine bottle by the neck, a not-so-veiled threat that she intended to conk him with it.

Tawny and Grace followed suit.

Under the table, Steph gently put a foot on Elaina's. Elaina took it as thanks. Steph then squinted so hard you could barely see the green of her eyes. "This wine club is about to *club* you if you don't get your slimy keister out of here."

Chapter Two

~ Burn Those Suckers ~

Face down, Elaina deadened a moan in her pillow. She shifted, trying to get comfortable and raked her teeth across her tongue. A tremor of revulsion quaked through her at the fur-like texture. Apparently, the wine she'd drank last night turned into fertilizer and she now had a lush landscape of fungi growing in her mouth.

Carefully rolling to her side, her eyelids drifted open only to be stabbed by an extreme ray of sunshine beaming through a tiny gap in the wooden blinds. The simple movement of closing her eyes made her temples throb. "Awesome," she muttered without moving her lips for fear it would trigger a bigger, more painful reminder of last night's foolishness.

A soft knock on the door made her jerk. "Arghhhh." She rose up and put her hands on her head to stop it from exploding.

Wait. A knock? She lived alone.

For a few long seconds there was nothing but silence. She must've imagined the knock.

Another low rap against the ornate six-paneled oak door made a seldom used expletive come from Elaina's mouth.

"Are you awake?"

Holy mother of…

Elaina scooted to the edge of the bed and threw her legs over the side. She stood up but teetered sideways, palming the corner of the nightstand. "Yes. I'm awake."

"Can I come in?"

Everything from the night before came back in a brain-cramping rush. Not only did she and the other members of the wine club send Stephanie's ex-snake a message to leave her alone, they also drank themselves silly. When it was time to head home, she was the one with the least blood alcohol, which wasn't saying much. They each had tried to drink their weight in wine. Elaina remembered shoving a wad of bills into the hunky bartender's hand for the commotion they'd caused and asked him to call a cab. Sometime after two in the morning, they ended up at her place. Instead of going to bed, they demolished a bottle of Moscato.

"Sure. It's unlocked."

Steph sauntered in looking like she'd been ran over by a road grater. Elaina was sure she had a road-under-construction look going on too.

"Do you have anything for a headache?" Steph rasped.

Elaina copped a chuckle, and it jangled her head like someone was bowling and had gotten a strike against her skull. "I'm not sure headache medicine is a good thing to take on an empty stomach."

Steph looked green around the gills. "Don't say stomach." She placed a hand on her belly. "Uh oh."

Elaina pointed to the bathroom a few feet away.

Steph's esophagus lurched and she sprinted past Elaina.

The sound of retching almost made Elaina do the same. She closed her eyes and took a few short breaths.

Grace popped into the room. "Oh good, you're up."

"Barely. Oh, you mean conscious."

"What did you think I meant?"

"Upright."

Steph came from the bathroom, ashen and holding one of Elaina's expensive cream-colored hand towels to her mouth. "I borrowed some of your mouthwash."

Elaina carefully nodded.

Steph eased onto the bed and curled into a ball. Grace sat on the corner of the mattress. Elaina parked on the opposite corner.

"We did a bad thing." Elaina jiggled with a small laugh. It gained speed and came out as a hysterical chortle.

Grace also cracked up.

"Stop bouncing the bed," Steph whimpered.

Elaina smoothed a hand across Steph's shoulder. "I know how you feel. Those annoying bowlers in my head keep getting strikes."

"What?" Steph was still a milky shade of pale.

Grace snickered. "I wonder what would happen if they got a gutter ball."

Elaina tried to stifle another laugh, unsuccessfully.

Steph winced.

Tawny joined them with a hand on her forehead. "Who's making the racket?"

Grace teasingly pointed to Elaina and Steph.

"Stop." Tawny found the only free spot on the bed and laid her head on the unused pillow. "Ahhhh" whooshed out.

"When you said 'toasted', you meant toasted. Dang, we funneled a lot of wine." Grace bent her neck from one side to the other. "I can't remember the last time I got smashed."

"Me either," Steph added in a barely audible voice. "It was long overdue. I might be sick as a dog, but I'm not sorry. I needed to let my hair down."

"Same here," Elaina admitted. "Running the gym and trying to deal with a broken marriage took me to the edge. I wanted to throttle anyone who looked at me sideways. After last night, I'm emotionally refreshed."

Tawny yawned. "Thanks to your new friends."

"And a shit-ton of wine." Grace moved off the bed. "I have to eat something. Do you have any bread? My belly is asking for toast."

"Toast for the toasted." Elaina motioned for Steph and Tawny to join them. "Come on, wine club. We could all use some toast."

Steph whimpered but dragged herself off the bed. "I hope the wine club is for real. I feel comfortable with you guys. Maybe we could meet on Friday nights?"

"I'm all for it," Grace said without hesitation.

"Let's give it a go," Tawny chimed.

"This feels like the beginning of something special. So yes, let's do this." They knuckled-bumped. "Aww hell, come here." Elaina gathered them in a hug.

* * *

"Who burns toast?" Tawny lifted her sunglasses and pushed them up on her head. Crossing her feet at the ankles, she leaned back in the chaise lounge. Her smile was huge and playfully mocking.

"They're not burnt. They're extra-crunchy." The plate of charred slices tipped but Elaina caught them before they fell onto the decorative concrete of the patio. "Okay. I burned the suckers."

Grace sat under the sun umbrella munching on a Granny Smith apple she'd snagged from the bowl of fruit on Elaina's kitchen counter. "Your culinary skills match mine. I swear I could burn water."

"I'm an awesome cook," Steph boasted, finally getting some color in her cheeks. "No brag, just fact." She patted her thighs. "I have proof."

Steph's self-deprecation was meant as lively banter but Elaina found it hard to make light of something she knew seriously bothered her new friend. "You know," she slathered peanut butter on a slice of toast, "the best way to get back at Corbett is to flaunt the best of you with an 'in your face' kind of thing."

"How so?"

Elaina inclined her head toward a room off the pool. "You mentioned you weren't happy about wearing sweat

25

pants. I have an exercise room here at home and I own a gym downtown. You can use either one, free of charge, anytime you want."

"You'd let me use your personal exercise room?"

"Yep."

"It would be awesome not to display my thighs for the whole world to see. I've had gym memberships in the past and I swear I've seen guys frown when I walked by."

"Or," Elaina emphasized, "it was your imagination. Maybe they were disguising interest by pretending not to be interested. Some guys are weird like that. My guess is they were checking all of you out, not just your thighs. You're an attractive woman, Steph. Your red hair is gorgeous."

"I don't want to sound like I'm beating myself up, but the cold hard truth is I'm overweight. I have no boobs to speak of. And my ex-fiancé paraded a goddess around last night to hurt me." Steph's voice splintered with emotion. "I need an extreme makeover."

Tawny moved from the lounge chair to the shade of the sun umbrella. "I need an emotional makeover to tune out the criticism I've put up with all these years. A breast reduction would also be nice." She adjusted her bra straps. "Realistically, I'm a pauper who can barely pay attention let alone reduce the size of these milk cartons."

Grace had just taken a sip of coffee and spurted it across the table. "Milk cartons?"

Steph joined them under the umbrella. "I'm begging for boobs and you're begging for someone to make yours go away. Life can be a cruel bitch." Her mouth drew into an impish grin.

"We come in all sizes. Big. Small. Tall. Short. Flat chests. Torpedo boobs. It's all good. Our focus should be health and loving ourselves enough to be happy with our bone structure and extra padding." Elaina winked at Steph. "Or lack of boobs."

"You're so lucky, Elaina. You're put together just right."

"Luck plays a small part. I work my butt off to keep my muscles toned and my weight under control. I actually exercise to the point of obsession. I know it, but can't seem to stop."

"How come?"

"I blame Arden. He repeatedly said I had to look the part of someone who owns a fitness center. I agreed, and I still do." Elaina bit into her toast.

"I want to look like you, only with red hair and green eyes. I want to be lean and gorgeous; for me, not Corbett. If the snake regrets tossing me away, it'll be a huge bonus."

"That's the spirit. I'll give you the security code to get into the exercise room. If I happen to be working out, you can use whatever machine is free."

Tawny perked up. "Can I get in on the action?"

Grace topped off their coffee cups from the carafe. "Don't leave me out. I want a smokin' hot body, too."

Elaina licked peanut butter from her bottom lip. "The offer is extended to the three of you." She motioned to the pool. "Bring your swimsuits. You can use the pool and enjoy the hot tub."

Steph slurped a sip of coffee. "This is quite the place." Her gaze skipped around. "I love all the plants and trees. It feels like a secluded mecca in the middle of town."

Elaina rapidly raised and lowered her eyebrows. "Arden wanted the house, but I stood my ground; which wasn't easy given his barracuda-like nature."

"Men," Tawny said with a thimbleful of enthusiasm. "You can't live with them and you can't spear them with a harpoon."

In the short time she'd known these ladies they'd replaced her dark mood with laughter and joy, and in a way, made her feel relevant. This alliance – or wine club – was exactly what she needed. Elaina held up her coffee cup. "To getting fit and smokin' hot bodies."

* * *

Grace hesitated at the door. "I was down in the dumps yesterday and I thought it would take a crane to haul me out of the muck. Then you showed up. Thanks for coming to my rescue."

"We rescued each other." Tawny shouldered Elaina. "Elaina gets most of the credit. If it wasn't for her, we'd be waking up to another gloomy, woe-is-me day with a little money in our pockets but our jewelry and memories already melted down." She made a face close to a frown. "My rings represent so many things, good and bad. I don't think trading them in for cash is going to fix what I have going on in here." She tapped the side of her head. "Until I can get my tilted world vertical again I'll hold onto them."

Elaina had come to the same conclusion about her rings but she didn't want to ruin the morning by delving too heavily into the subject, plus she was still suffering the side effects of an overindulgence of wine. "The only part I'll take credit for is the hangovers."

Grace leaned against the door frame and lifted her hand to display the platinum wedding set on her left hand. "I might hold onto these, or move them to my right hand and see how I feel." Her voice cracked. "You've given me strength and a new perspective. No one else has penetrated my gloom quite like you ladies did. Last night was fun. I'd do it again in a heartbeat, even if it meant another hangover."

"My stomach isn't done misbehaving but I'm happy as a lark. I haven't laughed so much in ages. Even with Corbett showing up and taunting me, it was a classic night." Steph put a hand up for a round of high-fives. "I'm going to give my mind and body a day off to recuperate, and then you'll see my ugly mug around here almost every day."

"I'm counting on it." Elaina had an idea bubbling up inside, begging to be shared. "Come and go as you like, but Friday night around eight I'll have wine and appetizers. Bring your sweat pants; not just Steph, all of you. We'll do something special with them."

Steph giggled. "I'm game. You might have to pry them off me though."

Elaina smiled.

"I'll be here," Grace confirmed.

Tawny said it was a date.

After exchanging cell phone numbers and a series of hugs, Elaina was left alone to deal with the emptiness of the four-bedroom, three-bathroom house that took up almost an entire city block. She'd heard people refer to it as a mansion. She looked around and wondered if she should've let Arden have it in the divorce settlement after all. It was a lot to take care of and too much space for one person. She expelled a lengthy sigh. As big as the place was, there were times it had felt as confining as a jail cell; usually when Arden had come home from the office in one of his grouchy, you-better-do-as-I-say moods. Now that she was on her own, with all the freedom to do whatever she wanted, in any room she wanted, she felt restless and lonely.

Chapter Three

- Get A Grip -

"Anyone ever tell you you're the whole package?"

Elaina didn't recognize the sweaty man who'd finished lifting weights and was blotting perspiration from his face with a gym towel. One of the other girls must've signed him up as a member. "Excuse me?"

"I said you're the whole package. You're tiny but buff. And those brilliant blue eyes beg to be noticed."

It had been forever since Elaina had been hit on and instead of being flattered, the compliment ushered in a blast of cold panic. Keeping her face void of expression, even though her pulse was doing a lap through her veins like it was running the Indy 500, she changed the subject. "How was your workout?"

The blond man issued a half-smile, as if he realized he may have overstepped. "It was rough since I haven't been at it for a while." He looked around. "I've heard good things about this place. My membership was up for renewal at the gym across town so I decided to give your place a go."

Elaina's pulse leveled out and the panic faded away. "I'm happy to have your business." She offered a friendly smile to the man who was attractive but in no way handsome. Perspiration continued to dot his forehead and curl the ends of his hair. She tried not to notice his unusually long eyelashes that were doing a slow, sexy blink over blue eyes a shade darker than her own but it was hard not to stare.

An awkward silence filled the foot of space separating them.

The guy shifted from foot to foot. "I forgot to scan in." From the pocket of his black Adidas shorts, he produced his membership tag and ran it under the laser scanner. The name Michael Rexx popped up on the computer screen. He looked from the screen to Elaina. "I'm Michael." His brownish-blond eyebrows raised a fraction of an inch. "I'm sorry as hell about the come-on."

Elaina was surprised by the apology and waited for him to say more. He didn't. Fumbling to say something that wouldn't make her sound easy or like a complete dork, she said, "It's okay."

"You probably get hit on all the time."

Elaina started to snicker but cut it off before it made things even more uneasy. "Actually, I don't."

Michael rubbed his chin. "I've been out of the game for a while so I'm sorry if I came off as a moron."

"No. You're fine." Elaina waved away the possibility to lessen his anxiety. "It was a sweet thing to say, but I prefer to keep things professional."

"Let's start over." Michael wiped his palms on the towel and extended his hand for a shake. "I'm Michael Rexx."

"Nice to meet you, Michael Rexx. I'm Elaina Samuels." Elaina could feel a genuine smile kink the corners of her mouth.

Michael's blue eyes sparkled. "Word around the locker room has it the owner of the gym is hot and recently divorced."

Elaina finally laughed. "Here's a bit of gossip." She cupped her hands around her mouth to whisper. "I heard she's taking a huge break from men, for say, a year or two."

It was Michael's turn to laugh and he also whispered his reply. "Between you and me, I don't put a lot stock in rumors. Besides, why would a gorgeous blonde take a hiatus from happiness?"

Elaina had no ready-answer. She was thankful when another member interrupted the discomfiting moment by wanting to buy a pair of black stretchy, tummy-control Capri's from the 50%-off sales rack.

"It was nice meeting you, Elaina." Michael slung the towel around his neck and headed for the locker room.

"I'm *happy* to have you as one of our newest members," Elaina said after him.

Michael glanced over his shoulder and their gazes connected again. "I'm *happy* too."

Their emphasis on the word *happy* made the other member crinkle her forehead, either with curiosity or bewilderment.

Elaina flipped back into business-mode.

After the transaction was completed, she busied herself by demonstrating the proper way to use the rowing machine to a member who was about as coordinated as a stick. From there, she addressed inquiries about the Tuesday night core-strengthening class. When things slowed down, she pulled up Michael Rexx's account to learn more about the man who'd made her nervous for a few minutes. Sitting back in the leather chair, she stared at the computer screen, agitated with herself for being fascinated by the attention he'd given. It was too soon to let anyone with bedroom intentions cross the imaginary moat she'd put in place when Arden moved out. Elaina had vowed to keep the drawbridge in the raised position until she was sure she wouldn't get hurt again. So, she was probably looking at forever. But she had to admit Michael Rexx was interesting. The part of her in charge of protecting her heart from further damage locked the drawbridge and tossed the key into the moat. It also issued a warning – *don't think about him.* Reaching for her phone, Elaina typed a quick message, smiled, and hit send.

* * *

"I came as soon as I got off work." Tawny took a seat at the kitchen table, her eyes wide with concern.

A minute later Grace plastered her nose on the sliding glass doors. Elaina waved her in.

"Everything okay?"

Before Elaina could fib that everything was peachy, Steph pushed open the doors and barreled in like she was hopped up on caffeine. "Traffic was crazy. There must've been an accident on Franklin Street and they routed everyone down Pierce." She continued to talk a mile a minute. "Work was nuts." Slinging her purse onto the counter, she plopped down on a chair. "Ten minutes before it was time to go home, the boss gave me a stack of scribbled notes he wanted me to use to compile a letter before I left. Can you believe the nerve of that guy?" She looked from girl to girl. "Time to pump the brakes and take a breath?"

"Instead of slowing down, you were speeding up." Tawny nudged Steph with her foot. "I thought you might blow a hose before you got it all out."

A round of laughter was followed by a round of wine glasses clinking.

Steph slurped a sip of Cabernet Sauvignon and continued to babble. "It's been one of those days. I hit the snooze button three times, dilly-dallied too long in the shower, caught every red light from my place to work, and walked into the office at five after eight. The boss has a thing about being late. Lucky for me he was tied up with a phone call or he would've read my pedigree. The madness doesn't stop there. At lunchtime I went to get my salad from the refrigerator only to discover I didn't bring it. I took extra time last night to throw together a healthy lunch for today and I walked off without it."

"You didn't make it here to exercise this week, Steph."

"I meant to get here but I had a mountain of laundry,

the shower was gross and needed to be scrubbed. The kitchen floor looked like a herd of cattle came through so I had to mop."

"In other words, you wimped out," Tawny teased.

"I seriously wimped out." Steph held up a finger. "But I ate better." She sounded proud. "I consumed an exorbitant amount of broccoli. I'm surprised my skin isn't turning green." She grinned devilishly. "I'm down three pounds."

"Atta girl!"

"Since I forgot my lunch, I had to beg some cheese and crackers from the boss. So I'm starving. Do you have anything here I can munch on?"

Elaina shook her head.

"You don't?" Steph started to get up. "Where's your phone book? I'll have something delivered."

"I have food, Steph, and I'm proud you're making good choices. I was shaking my head because I thought my day was weird. I think yours has mine beat."

Steph sank back into the chair. "What happened?" She squinted hard. "Did the barracuda stop in?"

"Thank the Lord, no." Elaina wet her lips with more wine. "I got hit on."

"No kidding?" Tawny propped her elbows on the table and laced her fingers. "Is it the reason you summoned us before our Friday wine club meeting?"

Elaina pressed her lips together and nodded.

"You freaked out, didn't you?" Grace asked.

"I'm ashamed to say I did. Not in front of Michael, thank goodness."

"Michael, huh?" Tawny raised and lowered her eyebrows. "Is he worth freaking out over?"

"He's not bad."

"On a scale of one to ten?"

"A solid seven and three quarters."

"Did he ask you out?" Grace licked her lips before taking another sip.

"Nooooo. I didn't give him a chance and I made it perfectly clear I'm out of commission for a good year or two. It was the funniest thing. For awhile we spoke in third-person."

Tawny snorted a laugh with a mouthful of wine, which came out her nose. "You're unique, Samuels. Instead of telling him to take a flying leap, you declined without hurting him."

"Why thank you, Westerfield." Elaina pinged the wine glass with her fingernails. "There's something I've been thinking about this week and I want to run it by you. You don't have to give me an answer tonight. Take time to think it over and let me know when you reach a decision."

"Can we eat first?" Steph was chomping at the bit for food and looked like she would eat the table cloth if she didn't get something soon.

"Yes, ma'am." Elaina went to the oven and brought back a large covered dish containing grilled chicken breasts and red skinned potatoes. She sat it in the center of the table. From the refrigerator she retrieved a crystal plate heaping with cherry tomatoes, celery and carrot sticks, cucumbers, and slices of fresh pear.

Tawny jumped up to help. "Where do you keep the plates and silverware?"

Elaina pointed to the far cabinet and the drawer beneath it.

"I thought you couldn't cook," Steph said.

"I'm not a total ninny when it comes to the kitchen, but darn close. This is my favorite meal and it's as fancy as I get."

Tawny passed out the plates. "Right now, it's my favorite too."

"I'd be happy to share my love for cooking sometime." Steph cut a small bite of chicken and popped it in her mouth. She smiled like it was the best thing in the whole world. "Darn tasty."

"Anything tastes delicious when you're hungry." Elaina smirked.

"This *is* yummy. Then again, I'm famished like Steph." Tawny drew her cheeks into a high, teasing smile. "Seriously, this hits the spot. Now what is it you wanted to say?"

Elaina took the time to enjoy a cherry tomato before she got to the heart of the matter. Hopefully, she wasn't jumping the gun with what she was about to ask. Laying her fork down, she shifted on the chair. "Here's the deal." She paused and swept her gaze from woman to woman. "This is a big house. Too big. I've tossed around the idea of putting it on the market but a part of me can't let it go. This has been home for fifteen years. It's really the only thing that has a piece of my soul." She modestly cleared her throat. "So...I find myself in unfamiliar territory."

Steph heaped more potatoes onto her plate. "How can your house be unfamiliar?"

Grace flicked her on the wrist. "She isn't finished."

Steph elbowed Grace in return. "Sorry."

"I went over each of our circumstances, several times. The four of us could stand to save our pennies. It's a weird thing to say given my hefty divorce settlement, but I'm not going to delude myself into thinking the money will last forever." She swiveled to Tawny. "There's a better than good chance you might inherit Stony."

Tawny's forehead crinkled in confusion. "Where's this going?"

Elaina paused, wondering if she should proceed. By the next beat of her heart, without directly answering Tawny, she finished the offer. "We want to work out and show our exes – and us – that we can look damn good in the aftermath of having our lives turned upside down. Grace said she struggles with going home to an empty house. Being alone sucks. I've admitted I don't take pleasure in cooking. Steph, however, enjoys time in the kitchen. What do you think about…?" What if they say yes? Worse…what if they say no?

Tawny took the reins. "You want us to move in?"

Emotion welled up inside Elaina. "It's a lot to ask, but I'm sure it would be beneficial on so many levels."

"But you don't know us. Not really. It might feel like you do, but you don't." Grace patted Elaina's hand. "We got hammered and talked smack about the men who," her voice shook, "left us."

Steph put a consoling hand on Grace's shoulder. "You

didn't talk smack about your husband. You only had kind things to say about him. We're the ones who trash-talked and said we wanted to tie cement blocks to our ex's feet and push them in the Auglaize River."

Grace's watery eyes smiled before her mouth had a chance. "I'd love to move in, Elaina."

"I'm happy to have you, Grace. I agree we don't know much about each other, but we mesh." She struggled with the knowledge she'd paid a lawyer to do a background check on them. If she didn't come clean, and they found out later, there would be a serious issue of trust. Clearing her throat, she began. "I have something I need to add. Please don't read too much into it." Elaina topped off her wine glass. "Before I came to the conclusion this would be a good thing, I made some inquiries. Legal inquiries."

A weird look flashed across Tawny's face. "You did?"

"This is an impulsive offer backed up with a little logic. I hope you understand."

"I completely understand." Tawny forked another piece of chicken onto her plate. "You can't have three psychopaths moving in. Just one. Me. When Grady pulls my chain, and he does quite often, I turn into someone who should probably be locked up until I calm down." She rested her fork on her plate. "I'm just warning you ahead of time. Do you still want me?"

"I do. You're not a psychopath. You're a woman who's not willing to take anymore crap."

"Sounds better than psychopath."

"So, another yes?"

"A hundred percent yes. I have to iron out some

logistics, but yes."

Elaina swiveled to Steph. "Do you want to join us?"

"I want to say yes, but I need time to sort through the pros and cons."

"There are no cons." Grace grabbed a carrot stick. "Unless you see the cement block thing through. You'll be the cons."

"What would we do with our stuff?" Steph asked.

"I've got it covered." Elaina pointed out the window to a steel building at the edge of the property. "Arden's man-cave. He was forever buying and selling vintage cars. He'd drink beer and polish cars. Or drink beer with his buddies while they admired his cars. I'm sure he mourned the loss of the building more than anything else. It's climate-controlled and an empty space going to waste."

"You've thought of everything." Steph still held on to her answer.

"No she hasn't. You have no idea how much Huskies shed. I brushed Stony every day and the house still looked like I hadn't swept in a month. Nothing says Grady will give him up but if he does I can't expect you to take him in. I have to figure out a plan."

"Stony is welcome. We'll deal with the hair when the time comes." Elaina never had a pet, not even growing up. She'd asked Arden if they could get a dog but he adamantly rejected the idea, saying they were dirty and tied you down."

"You might change your mind when you put on a pair of black jeans or wear a dark top. I'm just saying."

"Does he bite?" Steph asked.

"Only if you coat yourself with gravy." Tawny jiggled with a laugh. "He's a sixty-two pound baby who'd rather snuggle than chase rabbits or keep away strangers. He garners all the attention when we go to the park."

"I know I should forgo more potatoes but I'm still hungry." Steph stabbed a chunk of potato and brought it to her mouth. Before she enjoyed a bite, she laid it back on the plate. "I hate my weight. I don't hate Corbett, but I hate what he did. I hate how I resort to food to cope. But I love you ladies. If I move in, will you help me become a better version of me?"

Tawny and Grace instantly said, "Yes."

"I think you're pretty great already. If you want to make changes, we can provide the encouragement but that's all. Becoming Steph 2.0 has to come from you."

"Steph 2.0. I like it. You know what? I'm in. Let's do this."

Excitement poured over the table.

"We can make this work. There might be times when we want to clobber each other," Tawny took a section of pear, "but if we handle things the right away, none of us will end up with a goose egg on our head."

"I, for one, need space from time to time." Grace's happy expression turned reflective. "Sometimes from out of nowhere I have weepy moments and want to stay in bed."

"We'll give you the space you need." Elaina rubbed a hand across Grace's shoulders. "This is a big house with a big yard. You'll be able to carve out a place to be alone.

If we crowd you, just say the word. We'll back off. That goes for the rest of you, too."

"There will be an adjustment period, for sure. I hope you don't get irked if I do something without thinking things through," Steph said upfront.

"Just be you. We'll figure things out as we go." Elaina stabbed a bite of chicken, added a small piece of potato, and savored the happiness bouncing around the kitchen.

The air conditioning kicked on, reminding Elaina of one more thing. "Did you happen to bring your sweat pants along?"

Tawny and Grace shook their heads. Steph had hers handy since she kept a pair in the car.

Elaina refilled their wine glasses. "Let's take this outside. Arden had a swanky fire pit built for when he hosted parties for his clients. They liked to sit around the fire, drink beer, and talk about making money."

"We're going to drink wine and talk about making money?"

"Nope. We're going to start a fire, drink wine, burn those awful sweat pants, and give our wine club a proper name."

"I know exactly what we should call us." Steph put her teeth together in a toothy grin. "How about *No Sweat Pants Allowed - Wine Club*?"

Chapter Four

~ Gas Masks All Around ~

"How can one woman have so many shoes, Tawny?" Grace was clearly blown away by the four cardboard boxes labeled shoes in black marker.

"Contrary to those boxes, I'm not the one with the shoe fixation. Grady insisted I wear heels all the time. Not just any heels – stilettos. He said they made my legs look longer and gave the appearance I was in balance. Uh, not. Walking in those things was like putting an apple on a toothpick. I'm surprised I didn't topple over. I think Grady had a secret wish for me to break an ankle." She lifted her foot to reveal a pair of brown flats. "No more heels for me unless it's a special occasion, like a wedding or something."

"Guys should have to wear stilettos for fifteen minutes." Elaina rumbled with a laugh. "It's all they could handle."

"I love high heels but they don't love me. My feet are too wide and the fat oozes over the edges." Steph made a pouty face.

Elaina wrenched an arm around her. "You'll soon be wearing heels, comfortably."

"Next week?"

Elaina gave her a pointed look.

"How how long will it take me to lose thirty pounds?"

Elaina looked Steph up and down. "I'm guessing you weigh a hundred and sixty pounds, give or take a few."

"You're good. I'm at a hundred and sixty-two."

"It's what I do for a living. Here's the realistic and sucky part. You have two things working against you: your eating habits and sedentary lifestyle. There's a misconception about our metabolism being tied to age. What actually happens is it slows down when our level of activity gets sluggish. Lucky for you, I'm here to help you get moving again and to eat healthier."

Tawny brushed by them with a box marked knickknacks. "Can you do anything for my boobs? I'd like to drop a cup size or two."

"When you lose weight, you lose it all over. In your case, you'd have to lose a hundred pounds to ditch those things."

"I only weigh a hundred and twenty-five."

"Your only option, Westerfield, is to undergo the knife," Steph cackled.

"Not going to happen." Tawny groaned. "The only cutting going to happen is what I've been complaining about for awhile – my bra straps cutting into my shoulders."

"Speaking of knives, I could go for a steak," Grace said. "I haven't had one in ages. There's an awesome steakhouse on the fourth floor of the mall. Want to do dinner there?"

"My boobs make you want steak?"

"Steph said knife and I pictured a steak knife." Grace stuck her tongue out.

"I'm up for steak." Elaina hefted a box from the entrance of the building where Tawny earlier unloaded the things from her trunk. Carrying it to the far corner designated for Tawny, she stacked it on top of two other boxes.

"That's the last of it." Tawny dusted her hands. "I called my sons and gave them my new address. They're thrilled for me. I also texted Grady and gave it to him. He sent me a snotty reply about moving out of the apartment and breaking the lease." Removing the elastic tie from her hair, she gathered the thick brown tresses and a few rebellious wisps, and redid her pony tail. "When I told him I didn't have a lease, he called me a liar. I was ready to jerk him through the phone and pummel his skinny arse."

"I'm glad you didn't have to break a lease."

"My son thinks moving in with you is a good idea." Grace wiped a bead of sweat from her forehead. "He admitted to being worried about me. At nineteen he shouldn't be stressing out about his mom." She put an arm around Elaina's waist. "Thank you for inviting me here. I won't be alone and Cody can concentrate on his travels. I've rented the house to my niece and her husband. Most of what I brought here to store is sentimental stuff."

"I'm glad you're here, Grace."

Steph carried a laundry basket filled with odds and ends to her specified spot in the building. "I broke my lease, but I only got penalized one month's rent. I can live with that."

"Regarding the rules of the house…"

Tawny hip-bumped Elaina. "No smoking in the house, right?"

Elaina's mouth curved high. "I was going to say there are no rules. Now that Tawn' has mentioned smoking, we have one rule – no smoking in the house. We're intelligent women who don't need to be governed. We already know about boundaries and such."

Grace sought the water bottle she'd tucked beside her things and drained what was left in one long swallow. "Ahh." She crunched the plastic to lessen the space in the recycle bin and straightened a cockeyed box. "This liberal no-rules policy comes from Arden telling you every move to make, isn't it?"

"It may be a deep-seated response to Arden's totalitarianism, but it's also to show my respect and the confidence I have in each of you." Elaina checked her watch. "It's five-thirty, ladies. Let's get gussied up and make the men of Cherry Ridge eat their hearts out… while we eat steak."

* * *

"Get your hungry butts in here." Tawny pushed the button for the fourth floor at the same time a drop-dead delicious, dark-haired thirty-something guy joined them in the elevator.

His sexy brown eyes roamed over them as a group, and then he gifted each woman individually with a slow, spicy smile. Dressed in tight blue jeans and a plain black t-shirt, he could've easily walked off the pages of an Abercrombie and Fitch catalogue. He positioned himself with his back to them; feet wide apart and hands on his hips. It had to be a deliberate move to show off his scrumptious backside.

Tawny mouthed the word "Yowza!"

Steph licked her lips.

Grace coyly ran her eyes up and down him.

Elaina made big eyes.

Ornery and awestruck, Tawny rounded her hands like she was going to cup his magnificent buns.

From out of nowhere a strong, putrid smell filled the elevator. They looked from one another and Grace pointed to the guy.

The hunk had some nerve passing gas with them standing so closely behind him.

Tawny plugged her nose.

Elaina put a hand over her mouth and nose.

Steph gave him the *stink* eye for stinking up the tiny space.

The guy swiveled around with a mean look at the same time the elevator dinged open at the third floor. He stepped out and kept his scowl in place. "Really?" He didn't wait around for them to accuse him or to defend themselves.

Tawny fanned the area with her hands. "He's probably

laughing his cute ass off."

Grace coughed. "I thought I was going to pass out."

"It smelled like spoiled cabbage." Elaina chuckled. "We should carry a supply of those little white masks in our purses. Wouldn't it have been a hoot for him to turn around and see us with them on?"

"I could bring some home from the hospital."

Grace nodded in agreement. "Do it, Tawn'. Next time we're in an elevator with a hot guy we'll have some fun."

Steph was still sneering when they reached the fourth floor.

The elevator opened to the restaurant. At least a dozen people were waiting in line.

"I'll see how long a wait we have and give them my name." Grace headed for the hostess.

Elaina read the menu displayed on a whiteboard easel. "Tonight's special: six ounce tender-cut filet mignon topped with buttery shitake mushrooms, seasoned potatoes, romaine salad, and pretzel breadsticks for $21.99."

Grace returned with a smile. "It should only be about ten minutes." She inhaled. "My stomach started growling the second it caught the smells coming from the kitchen." Her smile gave way to a grimace. "There it is again."

"There what is again?" Elaina asked.

"The awful smell. Did the hunk get off on the third floor but take the stairs up to the restaurant? I don't see him but I sure as heck can smell him."

Tawny moved away from their tight circle. "Whatever

that is, it's making me queasy."

Steph looked down at her feet.

"Steph?" Elaina was careful to keep her voice low so it wouldn't draw attention. "Was it you?"

Still with her head down, Steph mumbled, "Disgusting, I know. I can't seem to stop passing gas. I've been eating broccoli till it comes out my ears and it's turned me into a tooting machine."

Tawny eased back in. "I hate to tell ya, it's not coming from your ears."

Steph raised her head. "Eating healthy gives me gas."

"You don't have to fill up on broccoli." Elaina didn't want to make Steph feel bad although she was having a hard time keeping a straight face. "There are less noxious choices." She gave her a shoulder bump. "Green beans. Carrots. Cucumbers. Tomatoes. Squash."

Grace didn't hold back. "You wicked, wicked woman. You let the hunk take the heat for dropping the stink bomb."

The moment developed into maniacal laughter. Those ahead of them turned to see what was going on which made things even funnier.

Chapter Five

~Bad Hair Day!~

"I'm springing for dinner and a bottle of wine. Something fruity." Elaina scanned the wine list. "Oooo, this one has ripe mango and papaya and just enough coconut to make you feel like you're watching the sun set on a tropical beach."

Tawny looked over the top of the laminated menu. "You don't have to buy."

"I want to. This is the first of many great days together."

Tawny closed the menu. "Let me word it another way. I'm not having the six ounce filet steak special. I'm going hog wild with the twelve ounce and I don't expect you to pay for my overindulgence."

Elaina raised her eyebrows authoritatively and kept them in the up position. "I'm still buying."

"I'm on a diet and you're having a big-ass steak?" Steph whined.

"You can have a big-ass steak. We can all have big-ass steaks." Elaina laid her menu aside. "Tomorrow we start fresh. I don't want to call it a diet, but that's what it'll be. We'll eat smaller portions of meat, fish and chicken, and pile on the veggies."

"We'd better stay out of elevators then," Steph said sheepishly.

Elaina hid behind the menu again. Breaking wind was normal and necessary. It was also disgusting and not something she found funny. In this case, it was downright hilarious and could only happen to Steph.

Grace guided Elaina's menu down with her finger. "Laughter is definitely the best medicine. We've had a lot of woe in our lives, but things are looking up."

Their waitress brought four glasses of water and a wire basket filled with garlic biscuits. "I'm Melanie. I'll be your waitress." She shared the evening specials.

"We've already decided," Elaina said.

"You're making my job easy." Melanie readied her order pad and started with Tawny.

"I'll have the guy over there. The good looking one with dark hair and sexy scruff on his face."

Melanie's eyes conveyed a lot with one bat of her eyelashes: she was sharp, quick-witted, and eager to play along. "Which one?"

"The guy in the fancy-smancy suit. Are those size fifteen shoes? Woo-wee! You know what they say. The bigger the feet the bigger the…"

"Toes?" Melanie sparkled with complicity.

"Yeah. Toes." Tawny pawed the table like a cat in heat. "What side dishes come with guys with long toes?"

"Cherries jubilee?"

Grace snorted, hitting her glass of water. She caught it before it fell into the basket of biscuits.

Elaina's view was blocked by Melanie.

Steph craned her neck. "I still don't see who you're talking about."

"The guy whose hair is mussed because the woman he's with can't keep her hands to herself." Being over-the-top and obvious, Tawny pointed. "He's the dude sitting with the blonde whose nipples are about to pop out of her dress."

Steph's green eyes glistened. "Uh oh!"

Elaina hoisted herself up to see what the fuss was all about. A giant hand might as well have reached out and slapped her. *No. Freaking. Way.* She slid back down and wrung her hands in her lap.

Grace picked up on the rash movement. "What's wrong?"

"Nothing." Elaina guzzled water from her glass.

"Something's not right. What is it?"

Elaina closed her eyes to stabilize. She felt lightheaded and her heart was thudding hard against her breast bone. "It's Arden. I know the spawn of the devil can dine with whoever he wants, but seeing him with another woman for the first time is hard." She knew it would happen; just not this soon.

Grace stroked her hand. "Just breathe."

Elaina questioned if the blonde had been in the background of their marriage the whole time? Or if she was his first taste of freedom? She stretched for another look. They seemed quite chummy. Not first-date chummy either. Was the woman the reason Arden dialed up the meanness to finish them off? Elaina was on the verge of losing it.

"Cancel my order. I wouldn't order the guy if he was the only thing on the menu." Tawny zipped a hateful look in Arden's direction. "Would it be a big inconvenience to move us to a table in the back?"

"We can't move," Elaina said steadfastly. "If we do, the barracuda wins again. As far as I'm concerned, he's done winning." She coaxed some much needed air into her lungs. "I don't suppose you could sprinkle his food with a little ground glass?"

Melanie scribbled something on the order pad. "I don't want to see the inside of a jail cell but I'm up for a harmless prank. He ordered his steak medium-rare." She glanced over her shoulder. "You're getting well-done, buddy. I'd drop it on the floor in the kitchen but there are too many eyes. But something could fall off the shelf; say a salt shaker without a lid. When he takes a bite of his baked potato he might need a garden hose to wash his tongue."

"You're getting a huge tip. I'm going to give it to you now as added incentive." Elaina pulled two crisp one hundred dollar bills from her purse and slid them across the table. "He's a prickly man who won't have a problem making a scene. So have fun, but be careful. I don't want you to lose your job over that weasel. Give him the perfect steak to keep the cook in good graces."

Tawny pulled a hair from her head and pressed it into Melanie's palm. "This could find its way to his salad."

"I feel your pain. My boyfriend ditched me a few weeks ago." Melanie winked. "As soon as I get your orders underway, I'm going to take out my latent anger on your unsuspecting ex."

"You're one hell of a waitress, Melanie." Elaina retrieved another hundred from her wallet. "He hates spicy stuff. If you have a jalapeno or habanero pepper laying around or some Caribbean jerk seasoning that needs to be used up, go for it. I would forever be in your debt."

"Dang," Steph cackled. "I don't want to make you mad."

"That's right." Elaina straightened her posture, feeling empowered. "Get on my bad side and you have no idea what might happen." She set a steely-eyed gaze on Arden. "If he could see those tufts of hair sticking up, he'd blow a blood vessel."

"Midlife crisis?" Melanie asked.

"Nah. He's been an asshat long before midlife." Talking smack about the guy who'd complained daily about *her* hair, the clothes she wore, her cooking, the way she arranged the furniture, and a billion other things, was invigorating.

"Well then, he's long past due for some get-even."

Melanie finished taking their orders, giving Elaina a moment to reflect on why she'd stayed in an unhappy marriage. It wasn't like he used his big…feet…in memorable ways. She took another look at the giant fool with giant feet. If she had any misgivings about their divorce, tonight removed all doubt. Arden could wine and dine all the women in the country, as long as he left her alone. Elaina refused to let him ruin a great meal. She would focus on the three incredible women who'd made her laugh more in a week than she did the entire time she was married. She amended it to include Melanie. *Four* incredible women who gave her hope.

* * *

Tawny threw Ferdinand into drive. "Want to check out the new dance club on Jefferson Street?"

Steph negated the offer. "I squeezed into these jeans and if I dance the button will pop. I could put out an eye."

Grace agreed. "I ate too much. If I shake my groove thing, the back of my pants will split open. I'd rather go to Elaina's place and relax."

Elaina twisted around with the seat belt still latched. "My place is your place. It's officially your home."

"Calling it home will take some getting used to. And I didn't want to flaunt my new digs." Grace's grin was worthy of a chuckle.

Elaina marveled at the woman beneath the black clothes. Grace was a vibrant personality who would no doubt keep things interesting.

Tawny tried again. "Dancing burns a lot of calories."

"Sometime soon we'll bust a move. Tonight, I'm taking a bubble bath, reading a book, and drinking wine. By the way, thanks for shielding me when Arden walked by on his way out. I wanted to puff out my chest and be all bitchy, but I'm so not ready."

"You'd do the same for us," Steph said from the backseat. "Melanie was a hoot. I almost split a gut laughing when Arden took a bite of his potato. He looked like he was going to throw up."

Rain began to dot the windshield and Tawny flicked on the wipers. "Mel was a blast. She couldn't be more than twenty-one but she's a wise little hen."

"Mel?" Steph said.

"Her close friends call her Mel," Grace teased.

Tawny's cell phone plinked with an incoming text message. She handed it to Elaina. "Check my message? I'd do it, but my night driving isn't the best. If I take my eyes off the road for a second we could end up in someone's front yard."

Elaina made big eyes. "If you can't see I should be behind the wheel." She read the message. "Umm, it's from Grady."

"What does the grouch want now?"

Elaina gestured to the Franklin Elementary School parking lot just beyond the red light. "Pull in over there."

"What's wrong?"

"Nothing's wrong. Actually, something's pretty great. Since we don't want to pay to fix someone's lawn when you get excited and take your eyes off the road, you need to park this buggy and give me the keys."

Tawny parked Ferdinand and dropped the keys into Elaina's waiting hand in exchange for the phone.

Elaina bailed out of the vehicle and scrambled around to the driver's side. In the short span of time, Tawny had read the message and her mouth hung open. Bracing for a burst of hysteria, she was shocked when Tawny quietly said, "He doesn't want Stony."

"Awesome, Tawn'."

"I've been lost without him. But he drops hair with every step. Seriously, Elaina, you don't know what you're in for."

"I told you Stony's just as welcome as you are. Got it?"

It must've finally sunk in that Tawny and the hairy mongrel were going to be together again. "Woohoo! I'd kiss you, Elaina, but people would talk." She clapped rapidly. "I love that dog so much."

"I can't wait to meet him."

Tawny was suddenly charged. She bounced in the seat. "Are we there yet?"

"Hang on." Elaina put the pedal to the metal. "It's time to reunite you with the love of your life."

* * *

Tawny released the latch on her seatbelt three blocks ahead of pointing to the red brick house on the corner of Eighth and Washington Streets and she was out of the car before Elaina brought the car to a complete stop. "I'll be back in a few minutes."

"Is Grady going to hassle you?"

"It's a given. I can handle it, especially knowing I'll be leaving with Stonewall Jackson Westerfield."

"You named your dog Stonewall?"

"Uh huh. When I tell him to do something it's like talking to a stone wall."

"Stonewall," Grace repeated, sounding thoroughly amazed.

"Stony – when he's not in trouble."

"Would it help if we came with you?" Elaina offered.

"Knowing Grady, he'll rescind the offer to spite me if you tag along."

"The bastard," Grace mumbled.

Tawny took off running and turned when she reached the porch to give them thumbs-up.

"You had the house to yourself, Elaina. How are you going to handle three more people and a big dog?"

"A big house is supposed to have a lot of people and a dog," Elaina said joyfully.

No more than five minutes lapsed from when Tawny left the car until Stony galloped down the concrete steps and into the beams of the headlights. It was almost as if Grady had been waiting to shove him out the door.

Tawny held the leash, but it was unclear who was leading who and under her arm, a large plastic tote.

Steph tapped Elaina on the arm. "Tawny wasn't lying. He's one big dog."

Grace seemed equally astonished. "Where on earth are we going to put him?"

"I assume he'll stretch across your laps."

"That might not be the best plan. I'm dressed in black. Remember?"

Elaina looked in the rearview mirror. "I didn't give it a thought."

"I suppose it's time to ditch the dark clothes." There was an air of surrender in Grace's voice.

Elaina jumped out of the vehicle to assist Tawny and silently said, "Halleluiah!" Maybe Stony was a blessing in disguise. A big, hairy blessing.

Chapter Six

~A Surprise Every Minute!~

"I can't believe Stony sat in the front seat on your lap."

"It was the only way to keep him restrained until we got home. He loves people and has an unusual way of getting to know them." Amusement coated Tawny's words. "He sticks his nose in places he shouldn't. Need I say more?"

Elaina drew her thighs together and splayed a hand in front of her lady parts. She extended her free hand, palm-side up to Stony. "Have a whiff of this instead."

Stony's cute black nose was hard at work, sniffing everything. He smelled Elaina's offered hand, her legs, her feet, and tried to work his nose past the splayed hand. When she kept him out, he looked up with question in his big blue eyes.

"You're a wuss, Samuels." Grace knelt down and spoke to Stony in baby-talk. He got excited and licked her face.

Elaina shuddered for effect. "I'm not a germ-a-phobe, but I'm not about to let him lick anything from my neck up."

"Who's a good boy?" Grace scratched him behind the ears.

Steph crouched beside Grace and Stony greeted her with some tongue action too.

"You know what he also licks, right?"

"Euw!" Steph hopped up, followed by Grace.

Stony nuzzled Elaina's thigh again.

"He likes you."

"He smells the piece of steak I dropped on my pants earlier."

"Nah. He wouldn't cuddle with you if he didn't like you. Animals have a keen sense about people."

"They also have a keen sense about steak."

Tawny rolled her eyes. "Let's go, boy. It's time for you to do your business and run off some excess energy before it rains harder." He made a weird noise, not quite a bark. It was a deep, throaty sound like he was talking to Tawny. She gave the leash a small tug and off they went.

Elaina was in awe of the close relationship. She giggled when Tawny tried to keep the upper-hand with the dog that was clearly in charge.

Hefting the plastic tote containing dog food and treats, she reflected on how things were changing by the minute. Last week the only sounds she'd heard came from the television, her heavy breathing from an intense workout, the unique clatter of the central air conditioning kicking on, and the gurgle of the coffee pot. Now there would be all kinds of noise – the commotion of friends and a lively pooch.

A loud clang drew their attention.

Grace held the door open for Elaina and Steph. "Either Stony wiped out. Or Tawny did."

"The way he takes off running from a complete standstill would yank my arm out of the socket." Steph rubbed her shoulder.

"There has to be a trick to keeping him in line." Elaina stowed the tote in a corner.

"You have to use a firm voice. When he ignores it, give him a treat. Although, if he misbehaves a lot, he'll be on a diet with me." Steph wandered to the cabinet for a glass. She filled it with water and chugged a healthy swallow. "I'm ready to drink myself thin."

"Water is essential, regardless of whether or not you're dieting." Elaina realized how nonstop she was with comments about health. It was a side effect of the day job. "I'm not telling you something you don't already know."

"I seriously want these thighs to go away, so crack the whip. Guide me to a strong, sleek body." Steph guzzled another drink. "I had an epiphany tonight at the restaurant."

"Induced by too much broccoli?" Grace ribbed.

Elaina crinkled her brows at Grace, and then grinned. "Sort of. I want a new me so badly I'm willing to eat foods that produce fumes." She pulled at her bottom lip with her teeth. "I'm going to stop bellyaching about what didn't happen with Corbett and look at the split as a good thing. He showed his bad self long before he ditched me. I was too in love with the idea of becoming his wife and I failed to see the real him."

"In some ways you described how things were for me

when it came to Arden. He was so good looking I chose not to see the side of him that would eventually lead to our demise." She winced. "The heart wears blinders sometimes."

"It's time to remove them."

"And we have to be careful not to judge all guys by the behavior of one." Elaina thought of Michael Rexx. His pickup line had been cheesy but it sounded like he was trying to regain his footing too.

"To stay on track, I'm throwing the entire male species into the off-limits category. I don't care how cute or charming they are." Steph refilled her water glass.

Elaina lifted the lid on the tote and found a dog dish, an opened bag of dry dog food, and treats resembling strips of bacon. "Someone needs to invent husband-treats for us to keep them in line."

Grace cocked an eyebrow. "Clip their balls and they'll behave."

Elaina and Steph exchanged looks of surprise.

"Grace Cordray," Elaina snorted but she was soon bent over, holding her stomach from laughing so hard.

Steph was laughing and dancing in place. "I'm about to pee my pants." She took off for the bathroom.

Tawny rapped on the sliding doors. Stony smashed his nose against the glass.

Elaina was still giggling when she flipped the latch to let them in.

"What did I miss?"

Steph hollered from the bathroom. "Grace thinks the way to calm down husbands is to clip their balls."

"What?" Tawny looked shocked.

Mischief etched Grace's face.

"You had to be here." Elaina ruffled the hair on Stony's head.

"The boss sprinkled every tree and bush. Your geraniums can't be the happiest of flowers right now. Stone-man knocked them over." Tawny shook her finger in reprimand. "Bad dog."

Stony hunched his shoulders and lowered his head.

"We might have to dog proof the house."

"I'm not worried about it." At Tawny's questioning look, Elaina added, "Seriously, I'm not. He'll get used to things."

"Anything he destroys, I'll pay for. You don't have any Ming vases do you?"

"No why?"

"Because I don't have enough money to pay for priceless works of art."

"Neither do I. So we're good."

Tawny filled the two-section dog dish with food and water. Stony lapped up the water like he hadn't had a drink all day.

"Give him a tour of the place to get him familiar with it. Nothing is off limits, including the basement." Elaina patted his rump. "Welcome, Stone-man."

* * *

Elaina stood under the massaging shower head, letting the hot water soothe the tender muscles in her neck and shoulders. She'd drawn tight when she saw Arden with his new woman and she was still all knotted up. Leaning her forehead against the wall of the shower, salty tears began to blend with the spray and anger tore through her chest. "Stop," she commanded. "Just stop. He's not worth it." She buried her face in her hands and wailed until she was limp from the overload of emotion.

From out of nowhere, something hit her smack dab in the butt crack. She lurched with a loud screech and almost lost her balance on the slippery tile. Putting a hand on the shower door to steady herself, she slowly turned. There stood Stony with water running off his fur, blinking droplets from his eyes, impassive to her startled reaction. Instinctively, Elaina put an arm across her breasts and one over her lower half. "What are you doing in here?"

Stony cocked his head at the question or perhaps at her less-than-thrilled tone.

"Listen, Stonewall, you need to keep your nose out of places it don't belong." Elaina cut the scold short. He was a dog, for crying out loud, not a real intruder. "No matter how determined you are to get to know me, this isn't the way to do it."

Tawny and Grace ran into the bathroom, breathing hard. "What's wrong?"

"I have a visitor," she replied calmly, "who sneaked up on me." She left out the part about him investigating her bottom.

"Stooooony!" Tawny pulled open the shower curtain. "I'm going to kick your butt! Get out of there! Now!"

Stony continued to blink water from his lashes but didn't move a paw.

"I'm so sorry." Tawny's chest rose and fell with a sigh. "I should probably record an apology. I have a feeling I'm going to be saying it a lot."

It took both Tawny and Grace to tug Stony from the shower. He tried to bolt the second he was out. Tawny wrapped her arms over his back and under his belly while Grace dried him – with a plush Egyptian-cotton bath towel Elaina had bought online from Crate and Barrel during a retail-therapy binge shortly after Arden left.

Grace held up the sea foam-green towel by the corners. "This is one of those my-bad moments." The towel was coated with white, grey, and black hairs. "In hindsight I should've ruined something less expensive."

Elaina yanked the shower curtain closed. "I'm going to have shower doors installed. Locking shower doors." She liked the homey look of a curtain but the blasted thing wouldn't keep anyone out.

"I forgot to tell you to lock the bathroom door. Stony loves to take showers. Most dogs would run the other way at the sound of a faucet being turned. Not Stoneman. He wags his tail and crowds in." Tawny looked around the shower curtain. "You could bathe a pack of dogs in this thing."

"Or I could bathe just me."

With the curtain still pulled aside, Elaina was on display when Steph entered the bathroom with her arms crossed, looking as if she'd been left out of the loop.

Elaina couldn't keep the scowl in place. "A little

privacy would be good here." A laugh was building, making her jiggle.

Tawny held Stony by the collar but he wanted no part of being contained. "Steph. Grace. Body him while I get his leash. He's still plenty wet. If he gets free he'll run through the house shaking off the water."

Once again, Elaina eased the curtain closed. She didn't proceed with her bath until she heard the click of the door.

Squirting a loofa sponge with plumeria body wash, she was mystified at the nonstop wackiness. With those ladies and that dog, life would be a surprise every minute. She'd be wise to occasionally lock them out.

Chapter Seven

~ Drop and Give Me Twenty ~

Steph charged into the exercise room with a towel around her neck, a bottle of water in hand, and a can-do expression. "Good morning, drill sergeant. It's day one of the new Stephanie Mathews." She stepped on the treadmill, sat the water bottle in the slot, and checked out the buttons. "Should I raise the incline?"

Elaina had just finished working her pecs. "How about doing some warm-ups first?"

Steph pointed both index fingers at Elaina. "You're the boss."

"Ha. Ha. Not."

"I'm serious. I need for you to boss me around like it's your day job."

"It *is* my day job. But I do a lot less bossing on Sunday."

"It was so cool that we went to church together this morning." Steph lowered her voice like she was spilling a secret. "I haven't been there in ages."

"Well then, going back can be part of the new you.

Although," Elaina smirked, "you might want to pay attention to the lyrics of the hymns before you sing at the top of your lungs. We're not supposed to laugh ourselves out of the pew when you sing the wrong words."

"I thought it said '*Had blinds but now I see*'."

"That's a different version of Amazing Grace." Elaina guzzled a sip of water. "We've all done it. It's funnier when it happens to someone else. And there's nothing wrong with singing your heart out. Keep doing it, chick."

"I think the snafu is the consequence of presbyopia."

"You need bifocals?"

"I scoffed when Corbett jabbed me about turning forty. I was fearless and ready to embrace my prime. 'Bring it on', I'd said. I swear at the stroke of midnight on my fortieth some crusty old goat sprinkled me with geriatric dust and my eyesight blurred. Son of a bitch."

Elaina purposely widened her eyes.

Steph put a hand to her mouth. "I just got out of church and I'm already cussing."

"I wasn't going to say anything." Elaina tossed Steph an exercise mat. "Come on, cusser, time to stretch."

On the mat, with her legs extended, Elaina reached for her toes. "Things aren't blurry for me, but I need some magnification when the print is extremely small. I keep a pair of cheater glasses in my purse."

"I've procrastinated going to the optometrist because he's a close friend of Corbett's. The first things out of his mouth will be to mention my age, scold me for waiting so long, and try to acquire breakup details."

"Get a new optometrist." Elaina demonstrated a hip

flexor stretch and motioned for Steph to follow her lead. "At the risk of sounding like a Hallmark card, old age isn't for sissies. The great thing is we don't have to go it alone. We have each other."

"You always put a positive spin on things. I prefer to grumble."

"You haven't seen me on a day when I wake up wanting to trip anyone who walks by. A pot of coffee usually fixes things." Elaina switched from her right knee to her left.

Steph also made the switch and teetered sideways in the process. "My balance isn't what it should be."

"We'll work on your core. Strong abs and back muscles are essential to balance. Your legs have to be toned too."

"I'm looking forward to being so toned you can bounce a ping pong ball off me." Steph rapidly raised and lowered her eyebrows. "It could happen."

"Yes it could." Elaina was fit but not to the point Steph was suggesting – few people were. It was a lofty goal for the serious-minded exerciser. If Steph wanted to achieve those kinds of results, Elaina would do her damndest to help make it happen.

"Did you notice I ate a piece of string cheese and half an apple for breakfast?"

"I did." Elaina had also watched her walk in place while she ate. "Do you have a pedometer?"

"I don't. Should I get one?"

"Not a bad idea. Put it on in the morning and take it off at night. You'll be amazed at how many steps you take in a day. Shoot for ten thousand."

"You know, Elaina, I'm not paying enough to live here. You're charging us next to nothing for rent and utilities. And you're giving free advice. I don't want to take advantage of you."

"I'm just tickled to have you here. Since you and the girls have moved in I've been sleeping better. After Arden left, I got a bad case of insomnia. Weird. With him gone, I should've slept like a baby."

"Getting a whole new life is great. How you got the new life, not so great. You probably couldn't sleep because your mind was busy doing what it does best – making folders for you to file and organize the past, present, and future."

"You're saying my mind was a messy desk?"

"Oh yeah. Big time clutter from your life with that…" Steph's grin was cheesy. "I was going to say shithead."

"You did say it."

Dressed in yoga pants and an overlarge Cincinnati Reds t-shirt, Tawny joined them. "I burned a lot of calories just thinking about exercising. Does that count?"

"If I have to sweat, you have to sweat," Steph quibbled.

Elaina dropped an exercise band behind her back and stretched it up with one hand and pulled down with the other.

"We could blow off conventional exercise and go dancing tonight. Hint. Hint. It's more fun and good for the heart."

Off the cuff, Elaina remarked, "Or really bad for the heart if you bump into your ex."

Grace wandered in with a cup of coffee and Stony.

"My workout is done. Instead of me taking Stony for a walk, he took me for one. It was actually more of a run to keep up with him." She slurped her coffee. "He's quite skilled at dragging me when I want him to slow down. I'm surprised I have any rubber left on the bottom of my sneakers."

Stony sniffed each woman before plopping next to Tawny.

Tawny pulled at the velvety tips of his ears. "Stone-man, take it easy on my friends."

Stony poked her with his nose.

"Sorry, ladies, I can't stay. Stony wants a treat."

Elaina used her best boss-voice. "Oh no you don't. Sit, Stony. Tawny, drop and give me twenty."

* * *

"Yes. I'm hot. Woot. Woot." Tawny pumped her palms in the air and strutted from the house dressed in a lime green two-piece swimsuit. The bottom fit aptly around her bottom and showed off fairly toned-abs. The top, however, was strained to the max trying to restrain the torpedoes.

Elaina lifted her sunglasses to take in the impromptu fashion show. "Stony's panting, but I doubt it has anything to do with your swimsuit. Do you want to go inside, boy?" He didn't move. She scrambled out of the chaise lounge. "You'll feel better in the A/C." He stayed put. "Obstinate male." She took a swig from her insulated water jug and then unscrewed the cap. "Ice cube?"

Now he was interested.

Stony wagged his tail. Beside him sat his dog dishwater bowl. Elaina emptied the contents of her jug into the dish. He lapped up the water, crunched on the ice, and looked for more.

Grace strolled from the house like she was also on a catwalk. She stopped in front of Elaina, did a slow three-sixty turn, and gestured the length of her. "Ms. Cordray is modeling a chic one-piece suit in black that subtly hides all her womanly imperfections. On her head, a floppy yet stylish straw hat accented with a black and white polka dotted band." She twirled a pair of chunky sunglasses. "We have to go shopping. Black is slimming, but clothes with color will improve my frame of mind. And I'm considering dying my hair back to its natural color."

Music to Elaina's ears. Grace was slowly doing away with the grief-garb. She'd even replaced black nail polish with soft pink. "What is your natural color?"

"Black."

Elaina shuffled across the hot patio in bare feet to refill Stony's water bowl from the outside faucet. "Tawn', I tried to put him inside. He didn't want any part of it. I think he's afraid he'll miss something."

Steph stepped from the house in a faded blue and pink flower skirt-type swimsuit. "Before you say a word, I want to go on record that I'll buy something nicer when I lose weight."

"Said every woman who decided to lose a few pounds." Elaina lifted her sunglasses to meet Steph's eyes. "We're shopping for swimwear this afternoon."

"And going dancing tonight," Tawny added.

Blech. Elaina didn't have an aversion to dancing. She had one for the whole bumping-and-grinding, what's-your-sign scene. To deter Tawny, she put her hands on hips. "Drop and give me twenty."

"Again?" Tawny's bottom lip jutted out in a playful pout.

Elaina snapped her fingers.

Tawny mocked with an eye-roll. "All that power is going to your head. Good thing you don't have a whistle."

Chapter Eight

~ Stretch It Out ~

Grace grabbed a hot pink bikini from the rack and held it against her chest. "What do you think, girls?"

"About what?" Tawny appeared distracted by something across the store.

Grace winked at Elaina. "The half-naked guy over by the camisoles."

Tawny's head snapped around. "What half-naked guy? Where?"

Steph craned her neck. "What were you looking at so intently?"

Tawny's brown eyes sparkled. "The clerk at the cash register. He's kind of dreamy, don't you think?"

Steph squinted as if it would help her zoom in on him. "The guy with the big ears?"

Elaina poked her in the ribs. "Be nice."

"I am being nice. He has elephant ears." Every inch of Steph's face was etched with mischief. "Poor guy. By the time he's eighty, those bad boys will be hanging to his shoulders."

Tawny frowned. "What?"

"The cartilage in your nose and ears never stop growing. And ear lobes elongate from gravity." Steph backed up with her palms raised. "I'm just saying."

Tawny frowned harder but the corners of her mouth quirked into a grin. "I wonder if the same holds true for feet." She stretched to look over Steph's shoulder. "What shoe size do you think he wears?"

"Uh, hello. What about the swimsuit?"

"Ixnay the hot pink, Grace. You're fair skinned. Try something in baby blue, tan, or even one of the jewel tone colors." Tawny still had her radar locked on the clerk.

"Jewel tone colors?"

Elaina knew the answer, but this was between Tawny and Grace.

Tawny drew her attention from Big Ears. "Amethyst, sapphire, ruby, garnet, citrine. You get the picture."

"Hmm. Citrine. Do I have anything citrine?"

Tawny amplified a sigh. "You're doing this on purpose, aren't you?"

"No I'm not. I must've been absent on color day because I seriously have no idea what citrine looks like."

"Oh for the love of Pete, Grace. You're brill'. How can you not know?" Steph said. "It's the color of quartz or a golden yellow."

Grace made a face. "You think I'd look good in golden yellow?"

"Get the pink," Elaina said. "You were drawn to it first." She checked the tags. "It's seventy-five percent off and if you use your credit card they'll take off another ten percent. You'll get it for next to nothing. If you don't like it, you're not out much."

Grace ran her fingers across the soft material. "I had a suit this color when I was in my twenties." She looked thoughtful. "The first time I wore it is the first time Brince and I made love."

"Even more reason to buy it." Elaina gave her a half-hug. "I'm going with this one." It was an odd shade; not quite pumpkin, not quite orange but there were metal hearts joining the fabric on each side of the swimsuit bottom. "Before summer is over, I'll have an outline of a heart on each thigh."

"You're such a dork."

Elaina hip-bumped Steph. "Takes one to know one." She sorted through the sales rack. "This is so you."

Steph turned up her nose. "Not."

"The olive-green will make your green eyes pop, Steph."

"There's nothing to it. I might as well prance around in pasties and a piece of dental floss."

Tawny stuck her nose in. "I'd buy a ticket to that."

"You're a bigger dork than Elaina."

"Want to know what I think?" Grace asked.

"It's not really a yes or no question. Is it?"

"Nope." Grace shifted in place. "My body isn't perfect but I'm still buying a bikini."

"Yeah. And?"

"The only people who'll see me wearing it are you three."

"I'm aging here. Make your point."

"Steph, we're your comfort zone. Buy the suit. You know you want to."

"I have stretch marks on my belly from gaining weight."

"Me too. Cody weighed a whopping nine pounds and five ounces when he was born. You can't give birth to a baby that size and not get a few stretch marks."

Tawny slapped Steph on the back. "Don't get me started on stretch marks."

"I've seen your stomach. There's not a stretch mark to be seen."

"I'm not talking about my stomach." Tawny pointed to her chest.

"Sheesh. Talk about peer pressure. I'll buy the damn suit."

Elaina noticed Tawny still hadn't done any serious looking. "Where's yours?"

"I'm good with the one I have."

"Taaaawny."

"I'm not dropping and giving you another twenty, especially in Macy's."

"The reason you're keying on Big Ears is to keep from picking something out. With a size seven bottom and a forty-two top, it's a hassle to shop. Am I right?"

Tawny's mouth parted in surprise. "You're too smart for your own good, Samuels. Yes, I hate shopping. Where you can simply pull something off the rack, I have my work cut out for me."

Elaina carefully chose her words so she didn't come off as sympathetic or condescending. "Do you know how many women would love to be built like you?"

Tawny drew a circle with her finger. "Zero. Zilch."

"Au contraire. When I sign up a female member at the gym, breast size is a big issue. Most women want bigger boobs and smaller bottoms." Elaina could read Tawny's uncertainty. "I wouldn't lie to you."

"There's a rack in the far corner with mix and match tops and bottoms. You might want to have a look," Grace stated.

"I'd rather have my teeth cleaned with a chisel."

Elaina looped an arm through Tawny's. "We should rename the club to No Wussies Allowed – Wine Club."

Ten minutes later, Tawny crowed with delight. She came from the dressing room stall to model the royal blue two-piece with tiny matching beads sewn on the bottom. "Women of Cherry Ridge, lock up your husbands."

A woman peeked out of the adjoining stall.

Elaina inclined her head toward Tawny. "She doesn't get out much."

"Hey. I heard that."

"Come on, windy, get changed. We have to check out the guy whose ears are growing as we speak."

In line to pay, Grace shared her opinion. "Close up he's kind of cute."

"Shh." Tawny put a finger across Grace's lips. "He'll hear you."

"How could he not with those ears?" Steph teased.

"I'm going to strangle you."

"I'm in no danger. You love me too much."

"Not."

"I know you do."

Tawny dropped the swimsuit on the floor instead of on the counter and was all thumbs when she tried to get her credit card out of her wallet."

"Don't mind her." Grace smiled up at the guy. "She gets flustered around good looking men. From her vantage point by the swimsuits, she could hardly keep her eyes off you."

The small space between his brows creased.

"Grace. Stop." Tawny's cheeks were a shade deeper than her blusher. She read the clerk's nametag out loud. "Dirk, please excuse my friend. She's a loon. And she drinks too much." She brought an imaginary bottle to her lips.

"Oh really?" It was an I-don't-know-what-the-hell-to-say response. Dirk held up Tawny's large swimsuit top to scan the tag. His eyes noticeably widened. He looked from the top to Tawny. Their eyes held before he cleared his throat and scanned the tag on the tiny bottom. He slid her card through the credit card terminal. "Thank you, Tawny P. Westerfield."

"You're welcome, Dirk." Tawny batted her eyelashes.

Steph turned to Elaina and pretended to gag.

Elaina looked away to keep from laughing.

Steph wouldn't let up. "What does the P stand for?"

Tawny was on her game. "Precious."

All of them, including Dirk, lost it.

* * *

"Sundays at the Westerfield house were never any fun. I swear Grady would pick a fight just so he could hog the television. I'm glad you liven things up no matter what day it is, Elaina."

"It's not just me. You girls aren't slackers when it comes to the funny stuff. My cheeks still hurt from laughing so much." Elaina turned onto Clay Street.

"Oh my gosh!" From the middle of the back seat, Steph leaned forward until she was almost in the front. "It looks like the ex-Westerfield is still trying to ruin your Sundays."

Tawny stretched to look around Steph and she let go of a string of cuss words.

Elaina pulled into the driveway and stopped short of the garage. "What in the world?"

"I'm going to pull his nose hairs out, one by one, with a pair of pliers."

There were some impressions in the yard indicating Grady hadn't bothered to use the driveway. He'd driven into the grass and dumped off Stony's big wire outside-kennel and a plastic grey kennel for indoors. A slew of dog toys had been tossed helter-skelter. A bag of rawhide bones rested against the front door. Elaina was pissed but she wouldn't pour fuel on Tawny's fire by expressing her displeasure.

"This is trespassing." Tawny's face was drawn tight and so were her fists. "He has no right to come on your property, especially onto your well-groomed lawn with his truck." She uncurled her fists to put them on her hips. "I don't get it. He was happy to get rid of Stony.

Why didn't he tell me to stop by to pick this stuff up instead of throwing it all over your yard?"

Grace gathered the toys. "It's not a huge deal. Right, Elaina?"

"Right."

"I'm not even here a week and he's making trouble for me." Tawny messed with the door on the bigger kennel.

"He hasn't made trouble for you. If anything, it verifies why you had to leave the doofus."

Pulling and pushing the metal on the bent door to try to straighten it, Tawny hissed and gave the kennel a swift kick. "In the mind of Grady Westerfield, I earned this special delivery by not kennel-training Stony. He nagged me to get it done. Between working long hours at the hospital and catering to his pampered butt, I didn't have the energy."

Mischief lit Steph's green eyes. "Are you up for a little payback?"

The corners of Tawny's mouth dimpled. "What did you have in mind?"

"I'm not sure. You'll need to give me some insight into what drives Grady nuts."

Grace came up with letting the air out of his tires.

"That wouldn't bother him. He has an air compressor." Tawny tapped her chin. "Let me think."

"We could puncture the tires."

Elaina kinked that plan right out of the gate. "We're not going to engage in criminal damaging."

Steph gave a good argument. "He damaged the kennels."

"It's not the same."

"I've got it." Tawny's angry brown eyes came alive with excitement. "He has a thing about textures."

"What? He gets the willies when he touches sandpaper?" Grace teased.

"Worse. He can't stand anything with a thick, pasty consistency; like axle grease or shortening. I wasn't allowed to make pudding or buy hummus. Chip dip was an absolute no."

"He's kind of a sissy-boy," Steph concluded.

"Definitely a sissy-boy. And he'll go spastic if we spread some grease or shortening around."

Elaina wagged her finger. "There is no *we* in this revenge plan. You're not participating. He'll suspect you right away."

"No he won't. The guys he works with know about his idiosyncrasies. They're forever leaving surprises on his car door handles or in his desk drawers."

Grace patted Tawny's shoulder. "Elaina's right. You have to keep your nose clean on this one or you might pay dearly."

Tawny whimpered.

"But I don't see anything wrong with you driving the getaway car."

"I'm going to rut *his* yard with the getaway car."

"No you won't. You'll park a block away."

Grace and Elaina grabbed the bent kennel and hauled it to the garage.

Steph and Tawny followed with the smaller kennel.

"I'm going to owe you big."

"Buy a bottle of wine to celebrate after we do our dastardly deed and we'll call it even."

"Deal."

Elaina thought back to when she played basketball in high school. When someone fouled her on the court, they seldom got caught. When she retaliated she got called for the foul. Hmm. Before they retaliated against Grady, she should probably arrange for bail money.

* * *

Shortly after eleven o'clock, with Tawny behind the wheel of Elaina's Cadillac Escalade they stopped at the corner of Ninth and Washington Streets.

"It's go-time," Grace piped from the back seat. "Are you ready?"

Elaina was having second thoughts. She could picture the front page of tomorrow's newspaper. 'Chamber of Commerce member vandalizes property'. But she couldn't back out. "I'm as ready as I'll ever be."

"My heart's pumping like crazy. Feel it." Steph put Grace's hand on her chest.

"Remember, Tawny, stay out of it," Elaina warned.

"So bossy."

"This isn't a fun night of mayhem. It's giving your ex his due."

"It's a fun night of mayhem for me."

Elaina shook her head. "Not helpful, Steph."

"Stop worrying, Mother Hen. I'll be parked on Franklin Street." Tawny drove away.

The commandos dressed in black hid behind a large oak tree, each armed with a pair of latex gloves and a Ziploc bag.

Grace pulled something out from under her shirt and slipped it on her face.

There was enough light from the lamppost across the street for Elaina to see it was a catwoman mask. It was the funniest damn thing. Laughter ripped through Elaina and she had to clamp a hand over her mouth to keep from giving them away.

"Cordray, you have a screw loose." Steph's whispered cackle echoed in the darkness. "Where'd you get the mask?"

"Remember when I said I brought a box of sentimental things to store in the building?"

"Yeah."

"It was in the box. The last Halloween that Brince was around, I wore it when we went through McDonald's drive-thru. The girl working the window screamed but gave me a free order of fries for scaring the heck out of her."

"You're nothing like I expected."

"Good. I like to surprise people."

"Shh." Elaina gave them both a flick. "The object is to get in, do the deed, and get out. If you two keep yapping we'll get caught for sure."

Darting from tree to tree like cat burglars, they surreptitiously crept behind Grady's house.

Elaina snickered without making a sound when the theme from Mission Impossible played in her head.

Grace motioned with two fingers where she was headed.

"What does that even mean?" Steph asked.

Elaina had caught on right away, but Steph's perception needed a serious squirt of WD-40. "It means she'll get the back door."

"Why didn't she just say that?"

"Because she… Never mind. Pick a spot."

"Okey dokey." Steph jerked her thumb in the direction of the garage.

Elaina about peed herself when a light went on in the house. Grady walked by the window and she ducked below it. When the coast was clear, she uncoiled from a crouch and tiptoed to the front of the house. She smeared Crisco on the mailbox lid and the handle of the screen door. She grabbed a glob and coated the welcome-mat.

Grace ran by, huffing and puffing. "I might've been made."

Steph was fast on Grace's heels. "I covered the trash can lids and his car antenna. I didn't have time to do the handles. I'll get them the next time."

Elaina brought up the rear. Giving Grady his come-uppance was a one-time thing, at least for her. Under her breath she mumbled, "It felt good to be bad."

Fleeing through the alley, they made a clean escape.

Steph tripped and fell, palms-first onto the stones. "Oww."

A dog barked somewhere in the distance, followed by a few porch lights being flicked on.

Elaina winched Steph up by the back of her shirt.

They were almost to the getaway vehicle and Tawny drove forward.

Between ragged breaths, Steph threatened to beat the snot out of her.

Grace bent over and rested her hands on her thighs. "You'll have to take a number."

They caught their breath and went after Tawny. Damn if she didn't move the blasted thing another fifty feet.

Chapter Nine

~ Grow A Pair ~

"We should start a revenge-for-hire business," Steph said with way too confidence.

"Just because we didn't get caught doesn't make us payback-specialists." Grace tucked the catwoman mask in her purse.

"I don't know about the rest of you, but this girl needs a drink." Elaina stuffed the latex gloves in the console.

"Coming right up." Tawny took them to the winery on the edge of town. "I'm buying."

Steph showed Tawny her injured hands. "I need to file a Workmen's Comp claim."

"I'm going to nickname you Random, Steph. The stuff that comes out of your mouth is so hit-and-miss."

"I got injured on the job."

"No you didn't. You fell in a hole after we left the scene of the crime," Grace mocked.

"See why I need a drink?"

As soon as they were in the winery, Steph asked for a Band-Aid.

The girl behind the counter smiled. "We have a lot of things. Band-Aid's aren't one of them."

Elaina requested red Merlot. It was a dry wine that was supposed to be intense with a velvety finish. She smacked her lips. "I prefer sweet but this isn't bad." She sat on a stool and tucked her feet behind the rungs. "I love how the wines are described," she said to no one in particular, and popped an oyster cracker into her mouth. The crackers were supposed to distract the taste buds when you moved from one sample to another. "Rich port wine, radiating sensuous berry and caramel aromas."

The winery employee introduced herself as Rachel.

Elaina liked her straight away. She was outgoing with expressive eyes and a fascinating southern twang. "Hit me with the sensuous berry, Rachel."

Rachel rinsed Elaina's glass. "I'm not sure how berries can be sensuous, but I sell a lot of this one." She popped the cork and poured until the glass was a third full. "Close your eyes, take a sip, and tell me if it's sensuous."

"If I close my eyes and take a sip, I'll probably pour it down the front of me."

"Maybe you should take a sip and then close your eyes."

"I'll give it a whirl." Elaina took a small taste and fluttered her eyelashes over her eyes. She dropped her head back and deliberately moaned. "Ohhhh that's good."

Rachel's eyes twinkled with merriment.

Grace shoved her glass at Rachel. "Give me some of that."

Rachel divvied out a sample to Steph and Tawny as well. "What are y'all up to tonight, other than tasting wine?"

"Getting even with my ex," Tawny spouted like it was something everybody did.

Elaina had just taken another swallow and choked at the admission. Grace whacked her on the back.

"Criminals always trip themselves up," Steph snorted.

"We're not criminals," Grace defended. "We're members of a wine club."

"Cool. What's the name of your club?"

Elaina mumbled behind her wine glass. "No Sweat Pants Allowed - Wine Club."

"Come again?"

"No Sweat Pants Allowed - Wine Club."

"Classy, huh?" Tawny snickered.

Rachel crinkled her forehead. "Why aren't y'all allowed to wear sweat pants?"

"It's mostly for my benefit," Steph clarified. "I'm going to lose weight and flaunt my hot bod in my ex's face. To keep me on track we burned my sweat pants."

"It's true. You can't make that shit up." Elaina was having fun and drinking too much wine. "Looks like we'll be going home again in a cab."

"Again?"

"Funny story." Steph propped her elbows on the counter and relayed how they met. "We now live together."

Elaina happened to look at Grace and almost fell off the stool. Grace was wearing the catwoman mask.

* * *

They wedged into the backseat of the taxi.

The rather meaty driver whose cab smelled like stale cigarettes and mildew clicked his tongue. "One of you needs to sit in front." He looked at Elaina. "I'm not going to bite…hard."

None of the others moved leaving Elaina to ride shotgun.

The driver turned out to be a complainer. He said the country was going to hell. His wife was a terrible housekeeper. His job didn't pay enough. Most nights they had take-out or something made in the microwave. Here was the zinger: people were stingy when they tipped.

He continued to drone.

Blah. Blah. Blah.

Elaina twisted around to look at the others. Their eyes were glazed over. She was sure hers were too. She mumbled under her breath. "Here's a sufficient *tip*: grow a pair."

"I'm sorry, what?"

Avoiding his eyes, she fibbed. "I said I have to wash my hair." Listening to him reminded her of Arden. The stars had aligned for her ex, but he was a whiner. He made money faster than he could count it, yet he was never satisfied or happy. Luckily, *she* finally grew a pair and took charge of her happiness – after he complained himself out of their house.

* * *

Stony loped into the kitchen with his tail wagging. He greeted Elaina with his unique howl and a warm, moist lick to her bare thigh. She still cringed when his tongue made contact but Tawny called them kisses so it was hard to shoo away his sweet-germy affection. Plus, Tawny brushed his teeth every day and sprayed his mouth with a doggie-type mouthwash. It was interesting to watch Stone-man patiently wait for his master to finish brushing her teeth so she could brush his. Elaina hadn't known many dogs. Of the ones she did know, none of them loved taking showers or had a penchant for toothpaste. Sure the toothpaste tasted like beef, but Stony had to endure bristles to enjoy it.

Elaina ran her fingers through the soft fur on his head and did something she saw Tawny do – tenderly draw her fingers from the base of his ears to the tips. For a few seconds, Stony was putty in her hands. The second he spied Tawny, he jumped up and left Elaina in his dust.

Slinging her purse on the counter, Elaina shared what she was feeling inside. "Best. Weekend. Ever."

Grace shoulder-bumped her on the way to the bathroom. "I'm in complete agreement. We had a blast and we're not in jail. Anyone up for another glass of wine?"

"It was a fantastic weekend. Becoming part of the wine club and moving in here, was a good decision." Tawny yawned. "But my butt is dragging and my pillow is calling. Come on, Stone-man, time to do your business and then we're off to bed."

"I can take him out." Steph grabbed the leash.

"Are you sure?"

"Of course, I'm sure. He's our club mascot." Steph hooked the leash to his collar. "Let's check out the stars, Stony."

At the sound of the toggle lock on the sliding doors being flipped up, Stony had his nose on the glass and his paws moving. Steph barely had the door open a sixteenth of the way and the eager pooch wedged through to the outside.

Grace returned to the kitchen. "He's a handful."

"Takes one to know one." Tawny winked. "None of us are slackers in that category."

Grace batted her eyelashes. "Speak for yourself." Rifling through the refrigerator, she came out with a package of Colby cheese. "We should probably have some calcium and protein to offset the wine."

Elaina took a slice of cheese and wolfed it down like she was starving.

"In my humble opinion, woman, you don't eat enough. You're a string bean with muscles." Tawny ripped a section of cheese and popped it in her mouth. Between chews, she asked, "Arden's doing?"

"He's affected me in more ways than I care to count." Elaina helped herself to another slice. "But it's time to forget the past and focus on the future. I'm going to start by making googley eyes at Mark Harmon."

"Oooo. Does his wife know?"

"Well yeah. NCIS. Hello." Elaina filled a glass with ice cubes and water. "I have the last five episodes on my DVR."

Steph returned, breathless. "How is it possible for one dog to pee ten times? If you had twelve trees he would've peed twelve times. I swear he has a bladder the size of a five gallon bucket."

Elaina crouched beside Stony. "You're an amazing creature with sweet blue eyes and a beautiful fur coat."

The mention of fur made Grace rub the front of her black stretchy pants. "He likes to share that amazing coat." She pulled at the fabric. "Look at these things, you hairy beast. I'll never get the hair off."

Tawny held out a piece of cheese to Steph. "Don't be dissing our mascot."

Grace bent down beside Elaina and apologized to Stony. "I'm sorry, boy. You're hairy but you're not a beast."

Stony licked Grace's face and Elaina shuddered.

"Time to recharge my batteries for a busy week ahead. I'm doing twelve-hour shifts at the hospital on Monday, Thursday, and Friday. I'll turn into a zombie on Saturday and Sunday. Lather. Rinse. Repeat."

"What about Tuesday and Wednesday?" Steph asked.

"Partly-zombie with a chance of meatballs."

Elaina shook her head with admiration. "I don't see how nurses handle such long hours."

"We run on empty a lot of days."

"I'll lighten your load by cooking some great food," Steph promised. "To keep the boss happy," she grinned at Elaina, "it'll be healthy fare minus broccoli."

"Excellent." Tawny drew Steph into a half-hug and kissed her temple. "You're an amazing woman. You all are." She latched onto Stony and waved goodnight.

Steph was the next to leave, followed by Grace.

Elaina dropped a cleaning tab into the dishwasher and started the wash cycle. She checked the doors to make sure they were locked and turned out the lights. Normally she left a couple lights on because it made her feel secure. Now that she was no longer alone, she flicked them off and hummed her way up the steps. At the top of the stairs, she paused to reflect. She wasn't a mom and no longer a wife, but she had three incredible friends and a dog who was winning her over a little every day. Life was good.

* * *

Elaina popped open an eye, trying to adjust to the darkness so she could see the clock on the nightstand. She groaned at the time. Three-o'clock. Stony might have a bladder the size of a five-gallon bucket, but hers was the size of a nickel. Needing to go woke her up but she was comfy and didn't want to get out of bed. She squeezed her eyes shut and rolled to her side hoping the urge would go away.

It didn't. In fact, the movement was as good as a poke to the bladder.

If she turned on the light, there'd be no going back to sleep. She knew the path to the bathroom by heart. Chest of drawers on the left. Nightstand and lamp on the right. Easy peasy. Elaina dropped her legs over the side of the bed. She took a step and bumped into something warm that made her lose her balance. Reeling out of control, she put her hands out in front of her. They hit the dresser and she bounced backward, striking her tailbone on the corner of the nightstand. "Aaaaagh!" Piercing pain radiated across her bottom and up her spine. She scrambled to turn on the lamp and almost knocked it over.

With the room partly illuminated, she identified the source of the stumble. Soulful blue eyes blinked up at her but he didn't move.

Alarm raced through Elaina; the pain in her rump momentarily forgotten. "Did I hurt you?" She ran her fingers upward from Stony's nose to his eyes. He didn't respond, other than to continue looking at her. Wrapping her arms around him, she whispered, "I didn't mean to hurt you."

Stony's fluffy tail wagged.

Elaina gently pressed against his ribs to check his reaction. He dragged his tongue across her hand. She took it as a sign he was fine. Her tailbone, on the other hand, wasn't. She graced his head with a smooch. "You show up in the most unusual places." She wondered why he wasn't laying on the floor beside Tawny.

With controlled movements she shuffled to the bathroom. Lifting her cotton nightshirt to inspect the damage in the mirror, she twisted and contorted every which way. She gave up when she couldn't bend enough to see the injured area.

Stony poked his nose into the bathroom.

"I gave you free reign of the place, so come on in."

Elaina gingerly sat down. Stony landed at her feet, his

wet nose touching her ankle. "I've never had a pet; not even a goldfish. So this is all new. Since you don't come with a manual I guess I'll have to learn the hard way. Lesson number one: flick on the light in the dark. That's actually lesson number two. Lesson number one: lock the bathroom door when taking a shower."

Elaina crawled back into bed. Stony brushed against the bed frame and dropped to the floor. She was tempted to pat the mattress for him to join her, but stopped before she did something foolish.

She lay staring into the darkness. Should she tell Tawny about the incident? She didn't want to be a stool pigeon but if she didn't share what had taken place, the others might be surprised in the middle of the night too and end up with a worse injury.

The mattress dipped ever so slightly.

Flicking on the lamp again, there was Stone-man with his head on the bed. It was almost as if he was asking her to keep quiet. Elaina tweaked the velvet of his ears. "Just because you've been neutered and no longer have a pair, I'm going to grow a pair and warn the others to be on the lookout for you. We all have to have a healthy respect for your presence."

Chapter Ten

~ Parts Are Parts ~

Elaina hobbled to the desk and lowered herself into the leather chair, trying to get a handle on a rather muddled morning. She flinched when Millicent Markward leaned across the counter with a probing look.

"Did a black cat cross your path?"

"You've noticed my Monday going to pot?"

"Hard not to. In the twenty minutes I've been here, the machines have staged a coup. Plus, you're not your cheery self and you're walking around like you have a yardstick shoved down your pants."

"I'm cheery." Elaina pointed to a fake toothy smile. "See."

Millicent's face took on a smirk. "Right."

It was a Murphy's Law kind of Monday. The moment she'd shoved the key in the lock to open the gym, things went downhill. A belt broke on one of the bicycles. The vinyl cushion on the leg lift machine ripped. Two treadmills stopped working. The load of wet towels she'd thrown in the dryer was still wet thanks to the heating element deciding to pick today as the day it would go on the fritz. A toilet in the Men's room overflowed. And somehow she managed to wear two different socks. They were similar but a member with a keen eye was quick to bring it to her attention. "Life gets nuts every now and then."

Millicent's penciled-in eyebrows rose high. "If a black cat isn't to blame perhaps a banana peel?"

"No banana peel and no black cat. It's a parts thing – both machine and body." Elaina expected the small talk to cease and for Millicent to walk away.

Wishful thinking.

Millicent came around the counter and spoke in a hushed tone. "I'm sorry to hear about your divorce."

While the termination of her marriage was a matter of public record, few people mentioned it – at least to her face. Elaina tried to appear unaffected by the intrusion into her personal life. "It wasn't meant to be, I guess." If she'd only been married a short time, the comment would've made sense. Since she'd spent well over a decade with Arden it didn't.

"I had no idea you and Arden split until I saw him cozying up to the woman who bombs around in that putrid pea-green car. You know who I'm talking about. The woman who never wears a bra and has…" Millicent put a hand over her mouth. "I'm sounding like an insensitive loon. I'm so sorry."

Elaina felt the burn of unshed tears. "No worries. Really."

"When I'm nervous I say stupid things."

Why would Millicent be nervous? Elaina dug her

nails into the leather arms of the chair.

"Do you remember the Christmas party the bank sponsored a few years ago for the businesses in town?"

"The one where Shorty Kettlinger drank too much tequila and passed out? I think he might've knocked over the hor dourves table."

"That's the one." Millicent lowered her voice even more. "There's no easy way to say this."

Elaina scooted to the edge of her seat. "Just say it, Millicent."

Millicent inhaled and puffed out the air. "Arden made a pass at me that night."

Elaina drew back. She stared wide-eyed at Millicent, trying to comprehend the news. "He made a pass at you?" That couldn't be true. Arden was the king of good behavior, at least in public. He instructed her before each community appearance or event on how she should behave. The rat bastard!

Millicent's mouth stretched wide with a grimace. "The only reason I'm bringing it up now, is to give you ammo should you need it. The man has a wandering eye. The same goes for his hands."

Elaina sagged. "He groped you?"

"He said it was an accident – only because I overreacted. I told him if he put his hands on my butt again I'd tell my husband. My hubby would've throat-punched him."

"I would've punched him in the throat, too, and I'm not one to get physical that way." Elaina wondered how many other women Arden had felt up. She closed her eyes, embarrassed that the one she'd loved and trusted had misbehaved with someone he barely knew. Opening her eyes, she masked the pain. "I know this was difficult but I'm glad you told me. I'd rather have a grip on the situation than forever wonder why folks are whispering when I come around." Her thoughts were becoming rabid and vile. If Arden happened to walk in, the fool would have a difficult time walking out.

"I didn't mean to make your morning even crappier."

Perhaps a black cat did cross her path.

It took monumental effort to scale back everything she felt inside, to lessen Millicent's worry. If she went into a rant about Arden, she'd close the door of information – not that she wanted to hear more, but she needed to know everything. "You didn't make things worse. You've given me a new perspective." She sat a little straighter even though every muscle in her body had gone slack. "Anyone who goes through a divorce can tell you there's an introspection period where you question everything that happened. Was I to blame? What could've I done differently to keep things from crumbling? As it turns out, it wasn't me who caused our marriage to disintegrate. It was him. All him." In that moment, Elaina got it. She wasn't responsible. So why did her heart and soul hurt like crazy? She knew the answer – because to guys like Arden, the most important things held no value. They were just parts.

* * *

Grace held the door open for Elaina. "How was your day?"

"It was kind of sucky. Yours?"

"It was a suck-fest, too. My drawer didn't balance." Grace emitted a groan. "I had to comb through every transaction to see where I might've messed up. It took me a good forty-five minutes I didn't have to find the mistake. Our supervisor always seems to know when we mess up. He keeps his distance but crosses his arms and glares. He makes us feel like we slipped the money into our purses. Why did your day bite?"

"Equipment kept breaking." Elaina was hesitant to tell on Arden. She would eventually share what Millicent revealed. For now, she'd settle for a soft cushion and a strong cup of coffee.

Stony ran from the family room into the kitchen and lunged at Elaina. She braced for impact by leaning against the stove. On hind legs he stood almost as tall as her. He licked her chin. He probably would've lathered her whole face if she didn't gently remove his paws and guide him down.

The only thing Stony did to Grace was sniff her honey pot.

"He really seems to likes you."

"I have no idea why." Elaina flipped open the plastic tote and gave him a small treat shaped like a steak.

Grace's gaze moved past Elaina and her eyes all but popped out of their sockets. "Something's wrong!"

On the counter sat two grocery bags. The contents of one lay scattered. A bag of frozen peas teetered on the edge of the sink while a carton of ice cream sat on its side, melting and trailing sticky vanilla down the front of the cabinets and ending in a pool on the grey tiled floor.

Without addressing the mess, Elaina and Grace sprinted up the stairs.

"Steph?" Elaina hollered.

"Steph?" Grace seconded.

Steph's bedroom door was closed.

Elaina rapped her knuckles on the door and leaned against it to listen. There was no response and no noise to indicate movement. "Steph, honey, what's going on?" Still no answer. She turned the doorknob and found it locked.

"Do you have a key?"

"Somewhere. But I'm not sure we should enter without permission. We said we'd give each other space."

"She should have the decency to tell us to go away. But she's not saying a word which is making me think bad things. What if she fell in the shower and knocked herself out? Or maybe she tripped and hit her head on the dresser. Or worse."

"Don't go there, Grace." Elaina wrung her hands. "Let's try one more time. If she doesn't answer she can kiss her privacy goodbye."

"Open up, Steph." Grace pounded the door with her fist. "If you don't, we're going to kick in the door."

"We are?"

Grace half-smiled. "Metaphor."

A weak "go away" finally met their ears.

"Nope. No way. Not happening. Open up or we'll

make toothpicks out of your door." Grace winked.

"You talk big for being a short little shit."

There was a rustle of blankets. The door creaked open a fraction of an inch. "I want to be alone."

Elaina contemplated shoving her way in.

Stony bounded up the stairs and nudged his way between Grace and Elaina. He forced the door open with little effort.

Steph stood in a wrinkled white cotton blouse and polyester black pants. Mascara was smudged beneath red, puffy eyes and most of the blue eye-shadow was gone from one eyelid. She turned away and walked to the window to avoid further inspection.

Elaina followed. "What's wrong?"

"My pathetic life has caught up to me," she replied in a shaky voice.

Mine too. Elaina tabled her anguish to help Steph deal with hers. "Can we talk about it?"

"I don't want to spoil your day."

"Trust me, you won't. We're here for each other, Steph. Remember?"

Crocodile tears streaked a path down Steph's cheeks. "I ran into 36D's at the supermarket. Talk about awkward. Come to find out, she's not a bad person; a little naïve, but so am I. By the heads of cauliflower we had a long talk. As it turns out, Corbett had been sneaking behind my back for six months before he broke up with me." She went into a rage, calling him a slew of vicious names before huffing loudly. "That spineless, no good hunk of human flesh didn't have the decency to be truthful with me or with 36D's. He told her he was free as a bird. She thought it odd that he never took her to his place. *Our* place. I filled in the blanks and she filled in a few. "Do you want to know what Corbett told her?" She sneered. "That I had as much sex appeal as a 2 x 4." Her voice broke. "He made fun of my flat chest."

Elaina wanted to beat the tar out of both Corbett *and* 36D's. Neither one seemed to possess a heart *or* a brain.

"36D's tried to make me feel better by saying his lovemaking skills are seriously lacking and she's not going to stay with him. I expect backlash from Corbett anytime now. Not that 36D's will throw me under the bus, but you and I know in the heat of an argument my name will come up." She sighed long and loud, like a tire losing air.

Grace handed Steph a tissue. "Corbett can come at you with all he's got, but he'll retreat in a hurry because you have back-up. The second he opens his yapper, he'll regret it."

Stony snuggled against Steph like he was declaring his allegiance, too.

Grace and Elaina wrapped their arms around Steph. "We'll help you cut the head off the snake." At Elaina's widened eyes, Grace added, "Figuratively."

Tawny burst into the room. "Why is ice cream dripping all over the kitchen?"

"Damn. I forgot about the groceries." Steph pushed away with more tears spilling from her eyes. "I was going to fix you a fabulous dinner."

"You can cook tomorrow. Tonight we'll order a pizza,

drink wine, and vent while soaking in the hot tub."

Steph looked beaten down and spent. "It's time to consider implants."

Elaina couldn't fathom someone putting what amounted to gel packs in their chest. "You know, Steph, they're just parts."

"I need those parts."

Elaina wasn't convinced fake breasts were the way to go. She wouldn't try to talk Steph out of them, but she would try to convince the gorgeous redhead that she was just that...gorgeous. "Consider what 36D's said about Corbett's lovemaking skills. He's obviously a rhino in a playpen. Rhino's don't know shit about boobs."

Steph's chuckle was small. "Thanks for that imagery. And for shoring me up yet again. After talking to 36D's, by the way her name is Jessi, I fell apart in the checkout line, in my car, in the garage, on my way upstairs, and for a good hour in my room." She sniffed. "I've cried so much my eyes hurt. So does my chest."

"Maybe you've hit rock bottom," Tawny said gently. "And there's only one way for you to go – up." She slid an arm around Steph. "Let me tell you a few things about boobs." She escorted Steph to the bed and motioned for her to have a seat. "When I was a teenager, I thought I was the coolest girl in school because I had a big chest. By the time I was in college I hated the darn things. They're uncomfortable all the time. In the summer, I get a rash under them. In the winter, they're cold. At forty-six I want them gone. Think about that, Steph. And remember what Elaina said about them being just parts because it's true. The Good Lord gave you a small chest. Don't mess with his handiwork."

Steph cupped her boobs. "These were on purpose?"

"Big boobs won't fix your life."

From the nightstand, Steph's cell phone rang. She grabbed it and growled. "It's the rhino."

"You don't have to answer. You don't have to do anything where he's concerned. But you do have to drink wine and eat pizza."

Steph opened a dresser drawer and tossed in the phone.

"That's one boob you need to cut loose."

Chapter Eleven

~One, Two, Cha-Cha-Cha!~

Elaina adjusted the front of the short, black dress with the low-cut neckline. She'd hedged on wearing the dress until she remembered the crack Arden made the day she brought it home. He'd said it was something hookers would wear. It had been an impulsive purchase on a day when she needed to feel feminine. Sure, it was a little risqué but it wasn't as dramatic as he'd suggested. Today when searching her wardrobe for something different, the dress whispered her name. The tags were still on and it begged to be worn.

Posing every which way in front of the mirror, she gasped with approval at the way the stretchy fabric hugged her figure. If Arden could see her now – all hookerish with red lipstick and four-inch shiny black stilettos – he'd have a coronary. But tonight wasn't about him. It was about her and stepping out of the box just a wee bit.

Grace strutted in looking quite different too. "Wow, Elaina!"

"It feels good to be in something other than workout clothes." Elaina was nonchalant with her inspection of Grace. Instead of stark black, she'd chosen a white gauzy sundress with gathered stitching at the waist. Black open-toe heels revealed bright pink polish on her toenails. White-gold bling in the form of a delicate chain with an infinity knot sparkled from her ankle. "Grace, you're a vision!"

Grace smiled coyly and crisscrossed her arms. "I don't know about this."

"The dress is completely you. Sexy but subtle."

"My boobs are showing."

"It's a tiny line of cleavage. Those things are safely tucked in."

"At my age, a nip slip would gross everyone out."

"You're not going to have a nip slip." Elaina misted her neck and wrists with perfume from Victoria's Secret.

Grace held out her wrists. "Spritz me."

Tawny looked around the door but kept the rest of her hidden. "I need your advice."

"On investing your hard-earned money? Or whether it's fashionable to let your armpit hair grow?"

Tawny rolled her eyes. "You're a better bank teller than a comedian, Cordray." Instead of moving into the room, she remained behind the door. "This outfit looked great in the catalogue but up close it's too hoochy-mama, if you know what I mean."

"Until you actually show us we won't know what you mean." Grace yanked the door and latched onto Tawny.

Tawny's two-piece ensemble – black leggings and

a shimmery top that barely covered her tummy – was eye catching. At first glance, the top looked silver…and slippery. When she moved it changed to a coppery color. It was one of those fun fabrics that messed with your eyes. "There's too much of me to be wearing something like this. Don't skirt around my feelings. Give it to me straight."

"I'll always be honest," Elaina said emphatically.

"Honesty is my middle name," Grace giggled.

"No it isn't. It's Vivian."

Grace stuck out her tongue.

Elaina gestured for Tawny to do a three-sixty turn. "I'm not gonna lie, your clothes say 'come-hither'. So do mine."

"You look classy, Elaina." Tawny blew out a puff of air. "I took a shot at being classy. Epic fail. The only way this top could look worse is if I went without a bra. Here's the kicker – I like the look but I'm afraid it's too much."

"This isn't the 60's. If you go braless, we'll hear the blare of the missile defense system being readied." Grace's face was wreathed with humor.

"Seriously, banking is where it's at for you."

"All joking aside, you look great."

"Thanks, Grace."

Elaina tucked a wayward strand of Tawny's hair behind her ear. "I promised you my truthful opinion. Here it is. You have big boobs. No matter what you wear those things are going to stand out. You can disguise them with something boring, which won't work because they're still right there for the world to notice. Or you can celebrate them with something exciting, like with what you have on."

"She's right, you know. Stop worrying what the world will think. Be you." Grace ran the slippery fabric through her fingers. "I like the top."

"If they have one of those disco balls I'll blind everyone."

Steph scuttled into the room. "What about balls?"

Elaina wrinkled her nose. "They're hairy and scary."

"Indeed. Why are you talking about them?"

"If you snooze you lose, Mathews."

Steph's bottom lip protruded in a pretend pout.

"Tawny's concerned her top emphasizes the obvious. And she's deathly afraid of balls." Grace didn't crack a smile.

"Sidonglobophobia?"

"What's that?"

"Fear of cotton balls. Don't ask how I know, I just do. By the way, the top works, Tawn'."

Elaina sat in the gold and brown paisley patterned arm chair by the window. "The more we're together, the stranger the conversations."

Tawny drew a heart with her fingers. "I love you, ladies. You boost my self-esteem and make me feel relevant."

"You're relevant – with or without glitzy tops." Steph fluffed the back of her hair and turned. "Do these pants make my butt look smaller? They should. I'm down another two pounds."

"You're an inspiration, Steph. You have your eye on the prize. And you look amazing."

"Thanks, Elaina." She pulled at the waist of her Capri pants. "A few weeks ago these babies would've choked my stomach."

Steph's soft mint top with a swirly pattern and rust-colored geometric print ankle-length pants were oddly paired, yet fashionable.

"You didn't eat broccoli today, did you?" Tawny teased.

Steph squinted but her green eyes still sparkled. "No I did not. Nothing turns off potential dates quicker than being gassed by noxious fumes."

"Potential dates?" Grace's expression flashed with alarm. "If I get hit on, I may punch someone."

If anyone was eavesdropping, they'd swear they were listening to a group of insecure teenagers not women in their forties. Elaina hung on that thought. Being single and starting over felt like they'd hit the refresh button on things they should've already weathered; things like body image, jobs, eating disorders, guys. The only thing they hadn't whined about over the last few weeks was pimples. "You're the boss of your space. If a guy moves in and you don't want him there, politely tell him to back off."

"I'm so not ready to deal with flirting and cheesy pickup lines."

"Be your own secret weapon. Chow down some broccoli." Steph playfully pushed Grace.

* * *

Sliding behind the wheel, Elaina slanted a smile at Tawny

who was riding shotgun. "Are we ready to burn up the dance floor until our feet hurt?"

"My feet are going to be just fine. These black flats might not catch the eye of any hot guys, but I'd rather be comfy."

"You don't need shoes to get a guy's attention. All you have to do is walk in the place," Grace stated matter-of-factly.

"Because of my boobs?"

Grace messed with her diamond-stud earrings. "Again with the boobs. Forget those things. There's more to you than your chest. You'll snag a guys' attention because you're a real looker."

"We're all lookers. With or without boobs." Steph's voice seemed magnified by the darkness; or she thought an earsplitting volume was necessary to make her point.

"Damn skippy." It tickled Elaina to hear Steph not take the boob-thing so seriously.

A few chuckles and silence settled in.

The more Elaina tried not be distracted by thoughts of Arden, the more he was present. Why? She had no idea. Maybe it was because he'd given his seal of disapproval to the dress. Or maybe she was using him as an excuse for not being fully on board with going to the club. Whatever the case, the slime ball needed to seep out of her brain so she could have a good time.

"Red light," Tawny yelled. "Red light," she repeated.

At the last minute, Elaina stomped on the brakes. "Oops."

"Act normal. There's a cop car parked on the opposite

side of the street," Steph warned.

"Normal? What's that?" Grace asked.

Two blocks from the club, Tawny piped up with a candid observation. "We're all fighting this in one way or another. Going dancing was my hare-brained idea, but I'm this close," she held up two fingers to show an inch in measure, "to jumping out of the car and going home."

"No jumping out of a moving car." Elaina thrummed the steering wheel with her thumbs. "At your age, you'll break a hip."

Tawny's half-glare, half-grin was illuminated by the street lamps. "Bitch."

Elaina snickered.

Steph bypassed the good-natured heckling. "We're apprehensive about the night life because we haven't been single in a very long time. Technically, I was single, but unavailable. Corbett and I didn't go dancing. We didn't do a lot of things."

"Tonight is about turning the page on the past." Elaina signaled with the blinker and proceeded into the nearly full parking lot. The SUV bounced across a speed bump. Then another. And another. Elaina grinned in the rearview mirror and caught hell from the peanut gallery.

"You're doing that on purpose," Steph grumbled.

Tawny laid a hand on her stomach. "Good thing I peed before we left home."

Locating one of the last few parking spots, Elaina squeezed the Escalade between the thin white lines. "Look out, world. The geriatric wine club has arrived."

A Chevrolet Camaro filled with guys took the space

beside them with the bass of their radio cranked up; making the Escalade feel like it was rocking.

Grace grabbed the back of the driver's seat. "We are soooo out of our element."

Tawny refastened her seat belt. "What were we thinking?"

"Turning the page, remember?"

"Riiiight," Steph scoffed.

"Get your terrified keisters out of my vehicle."

Steph held onto the arm rest. "If you want me out, you'll have to pry me out."

"I don't have a crow bar." Elaina waited for them to exit. When they didn't, she called them "Wussies," and headed toward the grey brick building decorated with neon palm trees. She dangled the car keys for them to see. Either they joined her or they had to find another way home.

A tall, brawny guy blocked the entrance to check I'D's. He gave Elaina the once-over.

She held up her driver's license. "I know I don't look twenty-one, but trust me, I am."

The abundant girth of the guy bounced when he laughed. "You're barely twenty-one."

"You sweet, sweet man."

Grace, Steph, and Tawny were suddenly there, draped in animation. What had happened or what was said in the short time since she left them, God only knows. But she could feel their excitement. She blinked up at the bouncer. "They're *not* twenty-one."

Wisely, he didn't offer a remark, but stamped their

hands and motioned them in.

"Mrs. Westerfield," a male voice said from behind.

Tawny turned. "Jakob York. How are you?"

"I'm fine, thanks. Hey, Bo and I talked for an hour on the phone the other day. He said he's coming home for a week in September. I can't wait to see the knot-head."

"Me too. He hasn't been home in a while."

It must've dawned on Jakob that the mom of his good friend was in a dance club. "Umm…"

Tawny smoothed the awkward moment. "We're having a girl's night out."

Jakob lifted his chin like he was deciding if he would stay, given the company. "Well, party-on, girls." One of his friends grabbed the back of his shirt and yanked him into the crowd.

Tawny's eyes skipped around the dance hall. "There's no one here close to our age, except maybe the owner. Aaaaand we're the only ones not in jeans."

"It doesn't matter."

Steph was ahead of them, snapping her fingers, singing, "One, two, cha-cha-cha."

"Nothing says old geezers quicker than cha-cha-cha."

"So much for having to pry her out of her comfort zone."

Grace humorously raised her eyebrows. "We adapt quickly."

"Yes we do." Elaina was secretly thrilled no one their age was there. When she danced like a throw-back to the eighties, only the twenty and thirty-something's would be busting a gut laughing. "Let's dance."

Tawny held Elaina and Grace back. "I'm not doing the cha-cha."

"We could do worse things," Grace spouted.

"Like what?"

"Pole dancing."

* * *

Elaina mimicked the moves of the younger girls until they squatted with their feet turned out, hands over their knees, and booties thrust in the air. She made big eyes at Tawny. "I'm not twerking."

Tawny grinned devilishly and squatted with her hands over her knees. "This may only happen once."

"Go for it."

Elaina took a bathroom break. While washing her hands, she studied herself in the mirror. All the planking and weight lifting had given her body definition. If it wasn't for the few lines crinkling the corners of her eyes and forehead, she might actually look twenty-one as suggested by the doorman.

Two girls burst into the restroom, laughing. It was easy to see – and smell – they were well under the influence of alcohol. One girl could barely stand.

"This-s-s place is overrun with old people. Did you s-see the woman with the big boobs? Damn! S-she looks…looks…like my aunt Marge, without the apron and orthopedic shoes." Cracking up laughing, slobber ran down the side of her mouth. She tried to swipe it away with her hand and missed.

"What's with the glossy top?" The girl who couldn't stay upright without holding onto the sink, laughed and hiccupped at the same time. "Who does she think she is? Tina Turner?" Fumbling with the zipper on her jeans, she swayed. "You might have to help me onto the toilet and hold me so I don't fall off."

Elaina squinted with reproach; not at the image of one girl holding the other while she did her business, but the ridicule of Tawny. Deliberately turning the faucet on full blast, she put her hands beneath it in such a way that cold water sprayed in their direction. "My bad."

On the way out, she heard, "She's one of them."

"Proudly one of them."

Weaving through the muddle of bodies, she made it to the bar at the far end of the hall without being mauled.

"Sup?" The bartender with the razor-cut hair streaked with fluorescent green and blue lifted his chin.

"I'd like something sweet."

He pushed up the sleeve of his white t-shirt to display skull and crossbones tattoos. "You can have me. I'm sweet."

"I was thinking more along the line of wine."

His eyes connected with Elaina's before they boldly moved to her mouth and eventually her chest.

Less-than-flattered, Elaina was slammed by reality. She was being ogled by someone half her age; someone that started his conversations with 'sup'. Rocking back on her heels, she said, "Moscato, if you have it."

He smirked. "Coming right up." He headed to the opposite end of the bar.

"Have you rescinded your no-guys-for-at-least-a-year policy?"

Elaina twisted around. "It's more of a guideline than a policy."

Michael Rexx's blond eyebrows shot up. "So there's a chance you might want some male company tonight or in the coming days?" Before she could answer, he added, "You look gorgeous."

"Not too shabby yourself." It was meant as an obligatory response to the compliment but it sounded flirty, even to her. Sliding her credit card across the bar to pay for the drink, Michael interrupted the movement. "I've got it and I'll have a Bud Light."

"Thank you." Elaina sipped the fruity wine and smacked her lips. "I've decided to amend the *guideline* to six months instead of a year." Wow. Her plan to keep men at bay for a while was quickly crumbling. She blamed his sexy blue eyes.

She was used to seeing Michael sweating and dressed in workout gear. Tonight he looked every bit the hunk in an olive-colored golf shirt and tight blue jeans. The pleasant smell of after-shave met her nose.

She fixed her attention on his moist lips, wondering how he kissed. Her gaze drifted up and Michael smiled like he'd read her thoughts.

"If I play my cards right maybe I can get you to toss the guideline in the trash."

"Yeah, that's not going to happen." Elaina flinched inwardly at the conviction she heard in her voice. Michael appeared unaffected but she still felt the need to sand the sharp edges of her candor. "It has nothing to do with you personally. It's just after living in Arden's shadow for so long, I need time to find out who I am."

"I understand. Really, I do. I've been divorced for eight months and I'm still not certain how this is supposed to go. The one concrete thing I cling to is that I'm Zoe's dad. She's eight, by the way."

"Aww." Elaina was a touchy-feely person and wanted to put an arm around him, but she was determined to keep body parts in check. Even the smallest physical contact could send the wrong message. It was too soon for anything that might lead to kissing…or the bedroom. "That's incredible, Michael."

"This is my weekend without her." He cleared his throat. "How about you? Any kids?"

Elaina shook her head. "My ex didn't want kids."

He studied her for an overly long moment. "It's not too late. You're what? Thirty-five?"

Elaina peered over her wine glass. "Add six to the number."

"I would've never guessed." Filling the small gap between them, he was close enough to say something beyond personal. "You're in optimum shape. There's no reason you can't have a child."

"That ship has sailed, I do believe. But thank you." To lighten the serious moment, "We have a dog. He's the cutest thing." She filled Michael in on Stony and the current living arrangements. She clinked her glass against Michael's beer mug. "To new circumstances."

"Would those new circumstances involve dancing

with a guy who could really use the company?"

"I stink at dancing."

"No you don't. I saw you move on the dance floor. You're graceful and sexy."

Elaina felt the heat of a blush stain her cheeks. "I'm a copy cat. I watched the others and imitated their moves."

"You did one hell of a job then." Michael's lashes swept over his eyes. "Two dances, then I have to go." He set his mug on a nearby table. "My alarm is set for five."

"What do you do?"

"I'm an independent trucker. Tomorrow morning I have to pick up a load of car parts and haul them to Detroit."

For lack of something better to say, Elaina said, "I'm sure it's a fun job."

"It pays the bills, and sadly, the alimony."

Elaina took another sip of wine and ran her tongue across he lips. "Come on, before I change my mind."

Michael reached for her hand. She pretended not to see and tucked it behind her back.

Steph met them on the dance floor. "Elaina loves to do the cha-cha."

Elaina teased Steph with the stink eye.

"Is that a fact?"

"Would I lie?"

Elaina bobbed her head up and down.

"No matter what you do, I'm sure it'll be incredible."

What a schmoozer. Elaina couldn't stop a smile. "Whatever."

To Taylor Swifts, *Shake It Off*, she did a fast version

of the cha-cha, making Michael and Steph laugh. The throng of younger folks backed away. It was a parting of the Red Sea kind of thing where she was in the middle of the dance floor acting the fool. Instead of turning beet red, the little bit of wine she'd had made her lift her chin and give it all she had.

* * *

Grace inched between Elaina and Michael. "That took kahoonies."

Michael's expression hinted at a grin but his mouth remained a straight line. He obviously knew when not to agree.

"Sometimes things pile up and the only way to deal with them is to misbehave."

"Meaning?" Grace's light blue eyes bored into Elaina, demanding a better explanation.

"It's the divorce thing." Elaina looked away.

"Sounds like a half-truth."

"You're a wise little bird," Elaina admitted.

"I had a hunch something was bugging you. The reason I kept my suspicions to myself was to let you work through – or not work through – whatever was ailing you. I was hoping you'd get it off your chest before tonight."

Michael stepped around Grace to stand in front of Elaina. He whispered. "I hope I'm not the one bugging you."

"You're bugging me all right. Not in a bad way."

"Excellent." His voice was low and seductive.

Elaina wanted to step on her tiptoes and kiss him senseless.

"Thanks for the dance. Goodnight, sweet Elaina."

"Where were you fifteen years ago?" was on her lips, but again, she kept things friendly instead of personal. "Have a good sleep. See you at the gym sometime."

"Soon. Very soon." Turning to Grace, he said, "She needs to laugh, cry, and talk. All three will work wonders."

Grace winked. "I'm on it, boss."

Swinging his attention back to Elaina, he repeated, "Soon."

Elaina cocked her head and watched Michael's rear view disappear into a wall of people.

"The man is hot in lust with you."

Elaina was set to argue but Grace put up a hand. "He is and that's that."

"He's disconcerting in so many ways, Grace. I want to kiss him and shove him away at the same time."

"I can see it in your eyes."

Elaina straightened her posture. "You have keen instincts."

"I pay attention. Let's go over there." Grace tugged her to a less congested corner. "This is a little better. At least we can talk without shouting. Anyway, there's clearly an attraction between you and Michael. Are you going to give it a go?"

"My body screams yes every time he makes eyes at me. I'd love to go out with him but at our age, there'd be a lot of swapping spit and tearing off clothes."

"You say that like it's a bad thing."

"He's a great guy who's been hurt. I don't want to get involved only to freeze up. It would be my issue but it would add to his hurt."

"If you're meant to be a couple, you won't freeze up." Grace smoothed a lock of Elaina's hair from her face. "He's not the only reason I pulled you aside. You've mother-henned Steph this week while your blue eyes said you have troubles of your own."

"It's been a rough week," Elaina admitted, "but this isn't the time or place to talk about it."

"We can leave."

"No. We can't." Elaina nodded toward the bar where Tawny was deep in conversation with a tall, dark-haired man who filled out his blue jeans quite nicely. Tawny's body language said she was receptive to him and no way would Elaina barge in or pull her away."

"It won't hurt to go outside for a breath of air."

"That I can do."

The moon was high in a cloudless sky and there was little traffic going up and down North Street. They walked until they reached Elaina's Escalade.

"We have a semblance of quiet, so share," Grace prompted.

Elaina backed against the SUV. "It's nothing earth-shattering and I should've been able to move past it, but I can't seem to let it go."

"You're being stingy with details."

"My not-so-nice ex is worse than I thought."

"Did he rough you up?"

"Not physically."

"I'm going to need a little more."

Elaina swallowed hard. "One of my gym members informed me on Monday that Arden groped her a few years ago."

The size of Grace's eyes doubled. "You've been carrying this around since Monday? Oh, Elaina, you should've said something. There was no need to suffer in silence. We could've helped you deal with the bottom feeder long before now." She enveloped Elaina in a hug.

A group of people came down the sidewalk, headed for the hall. One smart aleck hollered for them to kiss.

At that particular moment, Elaina didn't have the emotional wherewithal to tell the guy to suck eggs.

Grace had enough for them both and gave him the finger. "Who did the miscreant touch?"

"Millicent Markward and who knows how many others."

"Millicent's just now speaking up?"

"She didn't want to cause trouble."

"No wonder you're upset." Grace proceeded to call Arden a few choice names. "When you give someone your heart you expect them to handle it with care. I don't know the bastard but I'm pretty sure his bad behavior stems from having a small penis."

Elaina giggled and snorted. "I love you, Grace."

"I love you, too. Now let's get the others. It's time to get our middle-aged rumps home."

"Thank you. For everything."

"I'm the one who should be thanking you. I haven't

been this happy, mouthy, and expressive in a long time." Grace bumped Elaina with her hip. "I can't believe I gave that guy the finger."

"You're a surprise all the way around, Grace Cordray. A good surprise." Elaina knew her fractured heart would be just fine. Grace, Tawny, and Steph were the staples and tape she needed to hold it together and make it stronger.

"Let's cha-cha our way back inside."

"I've done enough cha-cha'ing to last me for awhile." Elaina unconsciously put a hand on her tailbone. She hadn't bruised it as bad as she initially thought but dancing reminded her to go easy.

Chapter Twelve

~ White Lies and Dark Chocolate ~

Grace stumbled into the kitchen in her nightgown and bare feet. "I'm staying home from work." She rubbed her forehead. "I have the onset of a migraine."

Stony rose up from where he lay curled in the corner, looked around, and put his head back down.

Tawny shrugged into a white lab coat. "Are you sure you're not playing hooky?"

"Ha. Ha. You're hilarious first thing in the morning." Graced headed to the coffee pot like she was on a mission. After pouring a cup, she shuffled to Stony and petted his head. "It's you and me today."

Elaina grabbed a glass from the cabinet, filled it with water, and handed it to Grace. "You might be dehydrated."

"It's going to take more than water to cure this thumper." Without relinquishing her coffee cup, she took the water and downed a few swallows. "You're bright eyed and bushy-tailed. Not to mention sweaty. Did you get up early to exercise?"

"My eyes popped open at five-thirty. I tried to go back to sleep but my mind wouldn't shut down long enough for it to happen. I took Stony out for his morning sprinkle, did the crossword puzzle in the paper, threw a load of whites into the washer, and did a half-hour on the elliptical. I still had twenty minutes to kill so I got jiggy with the rowing machine."

Steph came inside with a red face and perspiration dotting her forehead. She carried an empty Gatorade bottle and her iPod. "The drill sergeant kicked my butt this morning. She made me run and plank, and then we did sit-ups and crunches until my belly was on fire." She raised high cheeks at Elaina. "My body thanks you."

"You're welcome."

From the refrigerator, Steph snatched a sandwich bag filled with carrot and celery sticks.

"Carrots and celery for breakfast?" Tawny asked.

"At least it's not broccoli."

"You've got me there." Tawny grabbed her purse from where she'd hung it on a coat hook. "I need a vacation. These twelve hour days are taking a toll." She sighed. "See you around seven-thirty."

"Before you go, care to enlighten us further about the hot guy we had to drag you away from last night? As soon as we got in the car you faked being sleepy and when we got home you made a mad dash upstairs."

Tawny leaned to look at the clock. "Not much to tell. His name is Carter Payne. He's an overconfident car salesman who tried to sell me a new car. I told him flat out I couldn't afford one, and even if I could, Ferdinand would be lost without me."

"Did he call you a flake for being emotionally attached to your car?"

"He didn't call me a flake but he gave me a weird look."

Steph was in heckle-mode. "He was too busy thinking about pawing you." She wouldn't let up. "Are you going to rendezvous with him again?"

Sarcasm and impatience oozed from Tawny. "Again? I didn't rendezvous with him to begin with. I don't want to bump into him again and I'm NOT a flake."

"Ooooh. Testy."

Tawny narrowed her eyes. "I have to get going or I'll be late. The shift supervisor and I aren't exactly chummy. If I stroll in a minute past seven, she'll be at the desk tapping her foot." She headed to the door but glanced over her shoulder. "I didn't mean to get up in your grill, Steph."

"Not a problem. I was baiting you." Steph flashed a toothy smile. "I'm finally going to cook dinner tonight. Have your taste buds ready when you get home."

"You're an angel." Tawny made a swift exit.

Grace waited until she heard Tawny's car door close. "Anyone believe the malarkey about not wanting to see the car salesman again?"

"Not for second." Elaina took a bowl of strawberries, a carton of plain yogurt, and a pitcher of orange juice from the fridge. "She's battling the same demons we are – wanting the attention of a man, but also afraid to get it."

Grace planted her butt in a chair. "You said I'm keen on figuring things out. The same goes for you."

Elaina shrugged. "Some days my intuition kicks in. Other days, I can't get the gist of anything."

"You just described me. I zero in on stuff and think I know exactly what's happening. Two seconds later it's gone." Steph munched on a carrot stick like a beaver gnawing on a log. "I'm too young to blame it on menopause."

Grace stuck her fingers in her ears. "La. La. La."

Elaina made a face of confusion.

"Don't say the M-word in my presence."

Steph was still pumped up on endorphins. "Menopause. Menopause."

"You're evil, Mathews."

"Why does meno…" At Grace's glare, Steph stopped. "Why does the M-word make you crazy?"

"Because the thought of hot flashes, night sweats, dry skin, and loss of libido doesn't thrill me."

"Being irritable is also a symptom."

Grace made a low, feral growling sound. "Eat your carrots…silently."

Elaina took it all in. Tawny had been a tad grumpy. Grace supposedly had a headache. Steph was an early riser who liked to rib those who weren't. "Care for a smoothie?"

"Can I have one and stay on course with my diet?"

"You can. Berries are a powerhouse of nutrients. They're low in calories, high in fiber, and a good source of potassium to help you recoup from your workout. I'm only going to put in a splash of orange juice for tang and I'll omit the tablespoon of sugar the recipe calls for." Elaina tossed the ingredients into the blender and hit the blend button. "Once you get your metabolism revved, your body will burn calories even when you're idle. And when you drink something healthy but packed with calories," she held up the blender pitcher, "your body will burn them up before they settle in your hips." She filled three glasses.

"Practicing your speech for work?" Grace topped of her cup of coffee.

"Sure sounds like it. I can't seem to turn it off."

Steph tasted the smoothie and her eyelashes fluttered. "Sinfully delicious."

"Make something sinful for dinner, Steph."

"Oh I will. I'd tell you what it is, but I want you to be surprised."

"Does it involve dark chocolate?" Grace helped herself to a smoothie.

"It can."

"Awesome." Grace stretched her neck from side to side. "I'm going back upstairs to…play hooky."

Elaina gave her a pointed look. "Is there something we should know?"

Grace shook her head but winked on her way to the stairs.

"Oh no you don't." Elaina darted in front of her. "You don't have a headache. You're staying home for another reason."

"Wrong." Grace tried to step around Elaina.

Elaina motioned for Steph. "Help me."

Steph didn't need to be asked twice. She became a human fence, preventing Grace from fleeing. "Should we tie her to a chair and shine a flashlight in her face?"

Grace drew back. "Roughing me up won't make me talk."

"Okay then, how about this. Fill in the blank. 'I'm not going to work because…'"

Guilt flickered in Grace's eyes.

Steph stood with her feet apart and hands on her hips. "Even though it may seem like we're bullying you, we're not." Elaina pulled out a chair from the kitchen table. "No interrogation techniques, just conversation."

Grace remained standing, slurped the smoothie, and licked her lips clean. "Dalton James keeps bugging me."

A guy was the last thing Elaina expected to be the root cause; except for maybe the memory of Brince. "Who's Dalton James?"

"He's the reason for the little white lie."

Steph fished her cars keys from her purse. On the end of the key chain was a small blue flash light. She clicked it on and shined it at Grace. "Give us more, fibber."

Elaina rolled her eyes at Steph.

Grace batted away the flashlight. "He's a classmate who wouldn't give me the time of day in school. Now that we're older and," she made air quotes, "available, he thinks we should hook up."

Steph twirled the flashlight. "Are you attracted to him?"

Grace lowered her head but looked up through

her lashes. "I used to write Mrs. Dalton James on my notebooks."

Steph knelt down to meet Grace's eyes. "And now he scares the bejesus out of you because he's bald and has a pot belly?"

Grace flicked Steph on the forehead. "He's five feet-ten, has six-pack abs, and a thick head of dark hair with just a sprinkling of grey."

"Then what's the problem?"

"Stephhh."

"Grace wants to hide from Dalton even though she's still hung up on him after all these years."

"We both know that's not what's at play here."

"It was better than saying she can't give her heart to someone else when it still belongs to Brince."

"It will always belong to Brince," Grace said inflexibly and without hesitation.

"Your heart is big enough for two, Grace."

Grace closed her eyes. "I'm wrestling with the attraction I have for Dalton. It feels wrong but at the same time it feels good."

"Maybe you should have dinner with him. Be upfront that it's a test date. If he's a decent guy he'll understand where you're coming from," Elaina said softly.

"A test date," Grace repeated, as if mulling over the idea.

"Let him know he doesn't have to pass or fail; that it's about you, not him."

"Do you still have those notebooks?" Steph teased but her tone was gentler.

Grace opened her eyes to arch an eyebrow. "Oh my, look at the time."

"Good one. Take the focus off of you, by putting it on us." Steph flicked the flashlight at Grace one more time. "Play hooky but it's just stalling the inevitable. At some point you're going to have to face him." She checked the time on her watch. "Darn. I have to quit bugging you so I can shower before work."

"I've got to get moving too. I don't have to open up this morning, but I want to go in early to move some machines around and to go over a few things with the staff."

"Thanks for the smoothie…and for seeing through my little white lies to get to the heart of things."

"The truth shall set you free, my friend."

Grace clicked her tongue. "Who said that?"

"*I* did." Elaina cracked up laughing and flew up the stairs.

* * *

"What's she doing in the kitchen that requires locking us out?" Tawny had been home for half an hour, was still high strung but showing signs of exhaustion from a hectic day at the hospital, and in desperate need of something to eat. She flitted from the chaise lounge and moved the chair to a shady spot closer to the house. "Hurry up, Steph," she whined. "It's almost eight o'clock."

Stony was allowed inside; only because it was ninety degrees and he was wearing a fur coat.

"If she doesn't call us in soon I'm going to McDonald's." Grace angled her chair away from the glare of the sun.

"I could scale the trellis to get to my bedroom and scare the crap out of her by coming down the stairs." Elaina adjusted her sunglasses and used the latest issue of Woman's World magazine to fan her face.

Steph finally flung open the patio doors and motioned for them to come in.

"Halleluiah." Elaina was in the kitchen before the other two even thought about moving. The aromas of garlic, green pepper, cilantro and lime met her nose. She closed her eyes and inhaled. "Ahhh."

"I'll take that as a compliment." Steph waved steam from the blackened tilapia in Elaina's direction.

Not only did the pleasing smells grab Elaina, so did the mess. The neat freak inside of her bristled from the apparent food bomb that had gone off. Onion skins, the ends of asparagus, the inside membranes and seeds of green peppers, and packaging from the fish cluttered the sink and counter. Every pot, pan, dish, and utensil had been used. Bottles of spice were missing their caps.

Grace and Tawny stepped exaggeratedly into the kitchen.

The moment Tawny spied food, she put a hand on her chest. "Be still my heart and rumbling stomach." Sniffing, she smiled. "Couscous! I love couscous!"

Grace made a face at the couscous.

Steph held a serving dish under Grace's nose. "Sweet potato hash. Better?"

"Definitely better."

"Ladies, have a seat." Steph draped a white kitchen towel over her arm, acting all high-class restaurant-ish. "For your dining pleasure this evening, I'm happy to serve an array of fine dishes. The menu consists of: grilled tilapia, cilantro-lime couscous, sweet potato hash, asparagus spears, and sugar snap pea salad." Her cheeks pumped high with a smile. "Each dish is tasty but low-calorie."

"You're a rock star, Steph." Tawny plopped down in a chair and bumped the table with her knees, rattling the plates and silverware. "Oops."

The table was decorated with green cloth napkins and a centerpiece of short-stem daisies, while small plates at each setting held a scoop of lime sorbet and an interesting looking creation involving watermelon.

Elaina smiled with approval. "Chef Mathews is in the house."

Steph beamed with pride.

Grace inspected the appetizers. "I was bashing you for taking so long. I take it all back."

"Those are watermelon, mint, feta, and prosciutto. I was going to use goat cheese but I couldn't find any at the grocery." Steph crinkled her forehead. "You were bashing me?"

"Good-natured bashing."

"I said I could cook. I didn't say anything about being fast."

Tawny stole an asparagus spear from the bone china serving platter. She took a nibble. "You shouldn't be working as an executive's assistant. You should be writing cookbooks and have your own cooking show."

Elaina popped an appetizer in her mouth and moaned with delight. She slanted a smile at Grace and moaned louder.

Grace giggled. "You watched *Harry Met Sally*, didn't you?"

"Ohhhh yeahhhh."

Tawny playfully poked Elaina with her fork. "No moaning at the table."

"Speaking of moaning, Grace," Steph said, "I noticed you went to work after all."

Tawny looked perplexed. "What does moaning and working in a bank have to do with each other? Am I missing something?"

Elaina moved her head back and forth for Steph to leave it alone.

Steph couldn't take a hint. "Grace has a crush on a former classmate."

The amiable expression on Grace's face turned somber.

For a second Elaina thought she saw a flicker of fire as well. "Back off, Steph."

"We have to catch Tawny up."

Grace's face tightened.

"Not now," Elaina warned.

"Sheesh. I should've prepared crab. It would've fit the mood." Steph threw her napkin on her plate.

"No one's being a crab. This is a delicate issue for Grace. If she wants to recap her day, she will. If she's not ready, we have to give her room to sort it out."

Steph used the back of her hand to wipe her brow.

"We *all* have delicate issues. I thought the whole point of moving in together was to help each other with them."

Grace set angry eyes on Steph. "I appreciate your sense of humor, but not today."

"Why not today?"

Grace groaned.

Elaina connected with Tawny's gaze and turned a pretend key on her lips. Tawny mimicked the move. If a battle was about to begin between Grace and Steph, they wouldn't jump in until there was a certain amount of carnage.

"This morning you got all worked up over menopause. This evening you're…" The corners of Steph's mouth curled up. "I know what's going on and it only has a smidgen to do with Dalton James."

Grace dropped her fork onto her plate with a loud clunk. "You think you know, but you don't."

"Wanna bet?" Steph plodded to the refrigerator and returned with a clear dish filled with bananas sliced diagonally and drizzled with dark chocolate. "Here. This should help your PMS."

With no prior warning, Grace broke into a hearty laugh. "Oh my god, you're a hundred percent right." Drawing her shoulders together, she exhaled a lengthy sigh. "My monthly ogre has turned me into a crotchety hen. I've wanted to peck people's eyes out all day."

Steph backhanded Grace on the arm. "Be warned. If my calculations are right, I'll be pecking eyes out sometime next week."

With the tension identified, the fabulous meal

continued.

Elaina watched Steph load more couscous and sweet potato hash onto her plate until there wasn't any space left. She'd promised to keep Steph on track with her diet but with a fragile peace in place, now wasn't the time to mention portion control.

"By the way, Dalton didn't stop by today. Dammit all to hell. Hand me those bananas."

Chapter Thirteen

~ *Deal Me In* ~

Tawny came from the house carrying a tray with a pitcher of something pink and slushy, four glasses, a Milkbone dog biscuit for Stone-man, and a Ziploc bag stuffed with so many playing cards in it one more card would've burst the seams.

Steph lowered her head to look over the top of her sunglasses. "What's the pink stuff?"

"Something to keep us cool on a hot summer day." Tawny sat the tray on the patio table. "The girls at work were talking about wine slushies the other day, so I checked Google for a recipe. And voila! White Zin, ice, and raspberries." She tried to pour the slush mix but the mixture was so thick she had to spoon it into the glasses. "Since you're our resident food guru slash critic you get the first taste."

"I'm not a food critic."

Grace held the glass back when Steph reached for it. "Oh wait! I am a food critic."

"Thought so." Grace handed her the glass.

Steph took a taste. "Raspberry dances on your tongue while the wine is cunningly in the background."

"Who talks like that?" Tawny jested. "A food critic, that's who. Seriously, Steph, you should pursue a career in the culinary arts. You clearly have a passion."

Steph lifted her shoulders. "I've given it some thought but it's difficult to walk away from a sure paycheck."

"You're young enough to rebound if it doesn't pan out."

Steph scratched her head. "Forty *is* the new twenty."

Elaina adjusted the pink ball cap embroidered with a breast cancer ribbon. "It's never too late to pursue your dreams."

Tawny passed out the rest of the slushies. "Let's play cards."

Grace sat up. "What are we playing?"

"Hand and Foot. Do you know the game?"

"Nope," bounced from Steph, Grace, and Elaina.

"Well then, let me teach you something new. Gather round, ya hens."

"I hope it's not like strip poker. If it is, I need to put on more clothes." Steph slipped her feet into flip flops.

Grace spooned slush into her mouth. "I'm not removing anything."

"Yes, Hand and Foot is just like strip poker. Not." Tawny grabbed a handful of cards and started to shuffle. "It's similar to Canasta."

"I vote we go inside to play. It's too stinking hot out here." Grace looked from woman to woman to get a nod of agreement.

"No way. I get enough A/C at the hospital. They keep it so cold in there I walk around for twelve hours with goose bumps. It's nice to have the heat."

Elaina tossed aside the fitness magazine she'd had her nose buried in. "Read the rules and deal me in." She coaxed some slush from her glass with her tongue. "And keep these coming."

Tawny explained the rules of the game twice.

"For the first hand we need fifty points to be able to lay our cards down?" Steph held up a red three. "These bad boys are five hundred points against us if we get caught with them when someone goes out?"

"Yes. And yes. It's not as difficult as it sounds. Let's play a practice hand. Just so you know, once you get the hang of it, I WILL be trash talking." Tawny rubbed her hands together with a devious look. "It makes things more fun."

Elaina took no chances during the practice hand but still got stiffed with a black three, which only set her back three hundred points instead of five hundred. "From now on, I'm either going to win big or lose big. So look out."

"Ahhhh, the trash-talking has begun." Grace flung her straw hat onto a nearby chaise. "We should play for money."

Elaina had the door bells wired so when someone rang the bell at the front door she could hear it on the patio. She heard the chime go off, repeatedly. "Lucky for you ladies, some annoying person wants my attention."

"Salesman," Tawny said.

"Maybe it's Carter Payne," Steph heckled.

Tawny stuck out her tongue.

"It's most likely the UPS guy. I ordered one of those tall patio heaters. I know autumn isn't for a few months, but it was on sale. Be right back."

Elaina hurried around to the front. To her dismay, it wasn't the UPS guy. Dressed in a stylishly cut, stark black suit, Arden stood scowling with impatience. Tempted to sneak back to the patio before he saw her, she hesitated a few sends too long.

Arden cut her with a narrow-eyed look of disgust. "It's about time."

"I was out back enjoying the sunshine with a wine slushie. I wasn't sure I heard…" Elaina cut off the explanation. She didn't have to justify anything. "What do you want?"

"Do I have to stand here sweating or will you let me come in?" Arden muffled something under his breath that sounded like, "It's my house."

"I'm in the middle of a card game on the patio."

"Playing solitaire, huh?"

The edge of sarcasm made the fine hairs on Elaina's arms prickle. "I'm playing cards with Tawny, Grace, and Steph."

Arden's eyes hooded even more. "Who are Tawny, Grace, and Steph?" He backed away from the huge Boston fern hanging from a hook. "I hate plants."

"Yes, I know." It took monumental effort to keep from reminding him how he hated almost everything, especially the idea of her having friends.

As though he had every right to, Arden brushed past her and headed to the patio.

"Sweet," Elaina bit acerbically, but the word fell short of reaching his ears because his long legs got him poolside ahead of her.

Expecting him to slash her friends with sarcasm, Elaina was surprised when he acted like a decent human being. "What are we playing, ladies?"

Tawny glared straight away.

Grace didn't exactly scowl, but she wasn't overly receptive to his presence. "Hand and foot." She shuffled the cards.

Only Steph appeared the least bit interested. "How are you?"

Elaina assumed Steph's memory hit a snag.

Arden dismissed Steph by ignoring the question. "I hate to drag your host away, but I really need to talk to her."

"Host?" Steph's mouth formed an O when recognition fell into place.

Elaina warded off a smirk by humming.

"You're Elaina's ex. Arden Wellby Samuels," Steph stated matter-of-factly.

A muscle in Arden's jaw ticked. He turned to Elaina. "Can we please step inside?"

"You won't melt," rolled off her tongue. Before he could bite back, she made tracks to the house.

Arden entered the castle he once owned and turned into the same old critical king. "Are you freaking kidding me?" A deep frown creased his forehead. He pointed to the tote of dog food and the bowl setting beside it. "You have a dog?"

"You didn't see Stony resting in the shade?"

"Who the hell is Stony?" He opened the patio doors to have a look and glanced back at her. "A Husky? What has gotten into you?"

Elaina's temper was hanging by a microfiber. She inhaled to calm herself down. "Having a real life has gotten into me; one with plants, a loveable dog, and friends." She wanted to tell him that next year she was tearing up his precious yard for a vegetable garden, but he'd probably stop breathing. And resuscitating him with mouth-to-mouth wouldn't happen.

Arden's eyes never looked beadier. He crossed his arms and his lips thinned to the point they almost disappeared. "Huskies shed like crazy. I spent a fortune decorating this place with the best of everything and now it's coated with dog hair."

"Yep."

Arden's voice notched higher. "That's all you can say is yep?" It was easy to see he was one dog hair away from exploding.

Elaina wouldn't back down. If she wanted to speak in one-syllable words she would. "Yep."

"Where's the classy woman I was once married to?"

"I'm right here – classier and wiser than ever."

"Wiser? Right."

Elaina wanted to summon Stony and command him to bite Arden in the ass. "You have two seconds to state why you're here before I get back to my card game."

Despite the confident façade she kept in place, she was sweating like someone turned on a garden hose. "One…"

"I came to see if you'd consider selling me the house. It's too big for you." He tried, unsuccessfully, to remove dog hairs from his trousers. "I was prepared to offer you a million but now that the place is infested with fleas and a ton of hair, I'm reducing the offer to a half million."

Elaina laughed maniacally. Some of the laughter came from pure astonishment. The rest was caused by an overload of nerves. "Fleas? Oh my god, Arden, you're such a snob. Stony doesn't have fleas. Yes, he's a furball, but this is his home. You can take your offer and stick it where the sun doesn't shine. I'm keeping the house and Stone-man, and I'm not kicking out my roomies."

Arden's face turned a deep shade of scarlet and his nostrils flared. "Your roomies?" He took a step toward her.

Elaina was determined to stand her ground. "Tawny, Steph, and Grace."

The barracuda put what little self-assurance she had to the test by raising his haughty chest and drilling into her with his meanest look yet. "They're living here?"

She couldn't resist jabbing him one more time. "Yep."

"You're running a commune home?"

"Yep."

"You HAVE lost your mind. I'm going back to the judge to have you declared insane. I'll also get a court order to relocate you from MY house to the nut house."

"Go ahead and try," she said with deceptive calmness. "While you're there, they'll serve you with a court order for more alimony in light of the evidence that you're a groper."

Arden looked at her like she was daft. "A groper?"

Elaina moved her head up and down. "Women are coming out of the woodwork to tell on you." One had come forward, but he didn't need numbers.

"What are you talking about?" He advanced another step and the tone of his voice was as scary as a nail gun in the hands of a five year old.

Elaina didn't shrink back. "You're going to play dumb? Listen, Arden. If you cause me one ounce of trouble by trying to win back this house with your lies, you'll be in for the fight of your life. I'm no longer a weakling who will bend to your bullying." She was an inch from his face. "Got it?"

"Did those women put you up to this?"

"You mean the ones you groped or my roomies?" Elaina laughed without a trace of humor. "I suddenly have a backbone and you're trying to figure out who put it there?" She almost tapped his chest with her finger, but thought better of touching him. "I had a backbone all along. I just tried to keep you happy by not using it."

"What did I ever see in you?" He gave her a vile look and clomped his way to the front door.

"I have no idea what you saw then or what you see now. We were wrong for each other. Have a nice sterile life without plants and pets. Oh, and I saw you with your new woman."

Arden's mouth dropped open. Just as quickly he clamped it shut, grumbled something under his breath, and slammed the door on his way out.

"I wonder if your new woman knows you're anal." Elaina returned to the patio, shaking inside but pleased with herself for finally standing up to him.

Grace handed Elaina another slushie. "We contemplated overpowering the jackass and wrapping him mummy-style with duct tape."

"I wanted to strip him naked, hide his clothes and keys, and post pictures on the Internet."

"Stephanie Mathews, you have a dark side. I like it."

"What did he want?"

"Me to kowtow to him."

"You didn't, I hope."

"I did not." Elaina's mouth stretched wide with happiness and a sense of accomplishment. "Deal the cards."

Chapter Fourteen

~ The Ole Switcheroo ~

Steph turned down the classic oldies radio station currently playing, Hot Blooded by Foreigner, to remark she and Grace had the same taste in accessories. "Our purses are identical."

"We have exquisite taste."

"Since I can't reach around to give you a high-five, pretend I gave you one." Steph drove to the Chinese restaurant she'd bragged about for a week. "This place is a hidden treasure. They have dim sum to die for and their Moo Shu Pork will make you orgasm."

"You better not say 'Mmm' when you're eating or we'll know what's happening," Tawny teased.

Elaina snickered to herself. Food had never given her 'physical' sensations. But who knows, Moo Shoo Pork just might.

Tawny stayed on the subject of physical contentment. "I recently read in a health magazine that the lycopene in watermelon can give a Viagra-like effect."

Steph jumped in with some foods known to trigger

appetite – of a different nature. Oysters, avocadoes, chili peppers, chocolate, and mushrooms were supposed to be aphrodisiacs.

"Does Moo Shu Pork have mushrooms?" Grace asked.

"Yes it does. Those fancy wood ear mushrooms." Steph released her seatbelt and peeked around the driver's seat. "Are you in need of an aphrodisiac?"

Grace gave Steph a Karate-chop on the arm. "No. I have an aversion to fungi."

"Wuss."

"My Chinese name is Fungi Wuss," Grace cackled.

"My stomach is growling." Elaina placed a hand on her stomach in an attempt to keep it quiet. She'd had a small salad for lunch and a glass of water with a lemon wedge. If she didn't get some real food soon she'd be eating the roll of Tums in her purse.

Tawny sidled next to Elaina on the sidewalk. "MSG isn't good for you. Don't a lot of Chinese restaurants load it on?"

"Ask them not to." Elaina was restless and on edge. She wanted to blame it on having a skimpy lunch, but deep inside she knew it was something more. What exactly, she couldn't quite pin down.

In the dimly lit restaurant, Grace whispered. "They keep the lights low to trick you into eating fungi."

"Shush."

The hostess came to them with laminated menus and a huge smile. "Welcome. Booth or table?"

Tawny and Elaina spoke at the same time. Tawny said booth. Elaina said table.

"I win," Tawny boasted as the hostess directed them to a booth in the back of the restaurant.

"Whatever." Elaina slid into the booth first. When Grace glided across the vinyl next to her, Elaina felt closed in; restricted, like she needed to put her elbows out to make space. She'd had the same feelings earlier at the gym. She'd kept her members at an arms-length which was weird. Normally, she worked the floor; greeting each member by name and encouraging them to go faster or pump a little harder to get the most from their workout. Sometimes she'd walk around and share information about the benefits of drinking water or how eating protein a half hour after you're done exercising can increase your metabolism. Today, she'd kept her lips tightly zipped.

Tawny flicked Elaina's menu. "What are you getting?"

Annoyed. "An egg roll and a cup of hot and sour soup."

Tawny made a face. "That sounds disgusting!"

Elaina inhaled and exhaled so she wouldn't say something she couldn't take back. She was glad when Steph took a hold of the conversation.

"You'll love hot and sour soup." She rattled off a lengthy list of ingredients; some of which included wood ear mushrooms, shiitake mushrooms, tofu, and tiger lily buds.

Fungi Wuss made big eyes. "I'm not eating anything with mushrooms, tofu, or tiger lily buds." Grace pretended to gag.

"Tiger lily buds sound delicious," Tawny jested.

"You're a weirdo," Grace spouted.

"True that." Tawny eyed Elaina while ripping into her thumbnail. "Everything okay? You seem ouchy."

"I'm fine." Elaina was as far away from fine as she could be.

"Oh-kay," Tawny replied, not sounding even the tiniest bit convinced.

"I'm just tired." It wasn't a complete untruth. She *was* tired. Hopefully a good night's sleep would improve her disposition.

The waitress brought glasses of ice water and two porcelain pots filled with tea. In broken English she rattled off the evening special: fried rice with shrimp or chicken, egg roll, crab Rangoon, and choice of soup for $8.99.

Grace handed back the menu. "I'll take the special. It doesn't have mushrooms, right?"

"Right." With a half-nod, the waitress took the rest of the orders. She bent at the waist with a bow. "Be back soon."

Tawny poured tea into tiny, handless cups. She pushed a cup and saucer across the table to Elaina. Tea sloshed over the edge of the cup. Most of the spill was contained by the saucer but some landed on Elaina's white eyelet top.

She flinched from the scalding tea. "Ah!"

Tawny scrunched her face. "My bad."

Anger surged in Elaina but she kept it in check. No good would come from giving Tawny an earful. She blotted her top with a napkin.

The waitress returned with their cups of soup.

Grace and Tawny fell into a discussion about the unrelenting temperatures and argued whether it was the result of global warming. Steph dove into her soup like she hadn't eaten all day.

Elaina carefully spooned hot soup into her mouth, reflecting on why she was a total grouch. The only thing she could surmise was Arden's visit had gotten to her worse than she thought. And…these sweet but sometimes maddening women were in her space all the time. Something had to give. She clinked her spoon against the porcelain soup bowl to get their attention. "I've decided to go away for a few days."

"Awesome. Where are we going?"

"*We* aren't going anywhere. I'm going by myself." She could feel a lie coming together. "I've wanted to check into buying a summer house on Lake Erie. It's in the wish-stage right now but I want see what's available."

"You don't have to go to the lake. You can check the available properties on the Internet." Tawny nibbled on a deep-fried wonton.

"Let me put it another way. I'm going to check out summer houses because I need time away. I have a lot going on in my head and if I don't get it sorted out, I may implode."

Grace ripped open a packet of Splenda and poured it in her tea. "Are we getting on your nerves?"

Elaina brought her tea cup to her lips and blew away the steam. How could she answer truthfully without hurting their feelings? She took the low-road and fibbed again. "No."

Steph asked how long she'd be gone.

"A few days. Maybe more."

Tawny hurled an unexpected question. "Are you and Michael Rexx having a clandestine affair? And the jaunt to Lake Erie is really to frolic between the sheets?"

A laugh came of its own volition and some of the tightness in Elaina's shoulders released. "I wish."

"You do?"

"A night of lust and lattes would do a body good. But I'm not ready for anything that begins with an L."

"You evaded the part about a secret affair."

Elaina spooned more soup into her mouth and smacked her lips. "If we are having a secret affair, it's so secret even we don't know about it."

"Hold that thought. I have to pee." Steph grabbed her purse and headed to the Ladies room. Grace did the same.

"Since it's just the two of us, care to tell me why you're so uptight?"

"I don't know what's going on with me, Tawn'."

"Maybe you really do need lust and lattes. You know a good romp." Tawny shifted against the back of the booth. "I had a dream about Carter Payne last night." She tore off a section of Grace's crab Rangoon and popped it in her mouth with a grin. "We were getting it on in an elevator."

It was hard to stay grouchy with that image swirling around in her brain. "Did you get caught?"

"We didn't, but easily could have since the elevator door opened at every floor."

Elaina giggled. "I needed to laugh, so thanks."

"Happy to help."

Steph returned with her eyes about to pop out.

"What?" Tawny asked.

"Nothing," Steph said sheepishly.

"Was someone smoking weed in the restroom?"

Before Steph answered, Grace returned. "Did she tell you?"

Tawny leaned into the table. "Tell us what?"

Grace hummed and looked away.

"Graaace."

Grace remained tight-lipped.

"She's not going to tell us, Steph. It's up to you. What happened in the bathroom?"

Their entrees arrived.

Chewing a mouthful of fried rice, Steph teased with a smidgen of information. "The ole switcheroo happened, that's what."

"Not following."

"I grabbed the wrong purse. That's all I'm going to say." Steph brought another forkful of rice to her mouth.

Elaina pushed the fork away. "Not until you give us more."

"Bother Grace. She's the one with a Trojan Pleasure Pack in her purse."

If there was any latent tension in Elaina's body it let go. She laughed so hard she cried. "I'm beginning to think whatever can happen, will. Do you really have a box of condoms?"

"Hey, who messed with my crab Rangoon?"

"Not important. Answer the question."

Grace sucked in her cheeks, swallowed hard, and reached for her cup of tea.

Elaina shook her head. "Spill it, woman."

Grace rubbed her chin with her middle finger. "I was in the drugstore and there was a display of protection. It was an impulsive purchase."

"To say the least."

Tawny stabbed a chunk of green pepper and took a bite. "We were having a conversation along that line before you two came back."

"Why were you talking about drugstores?" Steph slurped from her tea cup.

"Not drugstores, goofball – sex."

"Ohhhh."

"I'm not the only one who's having intimacy withdrawal, huh?"Grace asked.

"Say sex, Grace. You're having *sex* withdrawal," Tawny made clear.

A guy at a nearby table must've tuned into the conversation. His eyebrows rose before a smile took the corners of his mouth. Elaina turned so he wouldn't get the idea they were looking for available candidates.

Chapter Fifteen

~ Old Habits Die Hard ~

Elaina was surprised when Steph stormed into the gym.

"I'm up three pounds! How is it possible?" She paced in front of the counter. "What am I doing wrong?"

"We can fix this." Elaina urged her to have a seat in the small room off the main exercise area. "I have to throw a load of towels in the dryer and then I'll join you. Help yourself to a bottle of water from the fridge."

"I burned my sweat pants, and for what? So I could gain weight? If this keeps up, I'll be changing careers all right, but it won't be to have a cooking show. I'll be a freak show in the circus."

The motto Elaina swore to adopt flitted through her mind: Not my circus, not my monkeys. "It could be water weight."

"Yet you're telling me to get a bottle of water from the fridge?"

"Forget the towels. Let's go." Elaina was thrilled her shift replacement, Valarie, had come in ten minutes early. "I'll be unavailable for a bit, Val. Do you mind covering?"

"Not at all."

"I'll add an hour's pay to your time."

Elaina followed Steph into the private room and closed the door.

Steph dropped into a chair with a groan. "Despite my efforts, I'm not losing."

"You've lost weight."

"I'm not seeing it."

Elaina sifted air through her teeth, wondering why a mere three pounds had thrown Steph into a panic. She grabbed a tape measure. "Muscle weighs more than fat but it takes up less space. You might be up a few pounds for that reason, but I'll bet you're down a few inches."

"I hadn't thought of that."

Elaina noticed Steph clenching and unclenching her hands. "There's more to this story than weight gain. Let's have it."

"Are you psychic?"

"If it gets you to tell me why you're nervous, then yes, I'm psychic."

"I've met someone," Steph blurted. "It's just at the crush stage, but oh my god, he's hot!"

Now it made sense. "Awesome, Steph."

"His name's Jack. He works the meat counter at the grocery. I wanted to get some chicken breasts for supper and there he was; handsomely dressed in white and smiling at me like I was the only one in the store."

Elaina fanned Steph with a weigh-and-measure document. "This mini-meltdown is actually about Jack?"

"Duh. Hello." Steph bit down on her bottom lip. "I asked him if he had any tricks to keeping chicken juicy." She snorted. "I was so dazzled I almost asked how to keep breasts juicy. At the last second, my brain kicked back in and said chicken."

"What did he recommend?"

"A dry rub." Steph picked at the polish on her fingernails. "He can rub me all he wants." She wrinkled her nose with amusement. "If anything comes of this attraction, he'll find out I already know how to keep chicken moist."

"He'll be flattered that you asked even though you knew."

"He's so dreamy."

"I can't wait to check him out."

"Give me time to reel him in before you prance to the grocery to see if he's as cute as I say."

"You know I'm going to have a look. But I promise to be discreet with my inspection." Elaina stretched the tape measure between her hands. "For your peace of mind, let's take your measurements and set some goals."

"The goal is Jack."

"Yes he is."

"Well then, let's get serious about meeting your original goal – thirty pounds."

Steph puffed out her cheeks and slowly expelled air. "It's going to be rough."

"Anything worth having usually is."

"Old habits die hard. It won't be easy to reprogram me."

"Maybe now would be a good time to mention portion control."

* * *

"Anyone up for a chick flick?" Elaina ran a wide-tooth comb through her hair and smoothed a tube of candy cotton pink gloss across her lips.

"Not me. I'm headed to the treadmill." Steph winced. "If I'm going to get these thighs and my tush in shape I need to put in the time."

"Excellent, Steph. How about you, Grace?"

"I'm going to be a fuddy-duddy and stay home." She held up the latest book by Nora Roberts. "Nora and I have some catching up to do."

"Is Tawny upstairs or did she take Stony for a walk?"

Grace popped the tab on a can of diet Coke. "Upstairs, I think."

Elaina took the stairs two at a time. "Tawny, you up here?" She expected Stony to come running like he always did when she hollered. He didn't. Knocking on Tawny's door, she waited. When there was no response, she knocked again. "Tawn', you in there?"

"Umm, just a minute."

Instead of a minute, it was more like five. Elaina's gut instinct said something wasn't quite right.

The door cracked open, allowing only a sliver of Tawny to be seen. "Yeah?"

Hmm. "I'm headed to the theater to watch a sappy chick flick. You game?" The smell of cigarettes met

Elaina's nose.

"Some other time, okay?"

"Can I come in?"

Tawny yawned. "I was about to go bed."

"At eight-thirty?"

"I'm beat."

Elaina stuck her foot in the doorway so Tawny couldn't close her out.

Tawny grunted with something akin to accepting the inevitable. "Come in."

There wasn't a hint of smoke hanging around the room, there was a cloud. Elaina was instantly pissed. "When you moved in, I asked you not to smoke in the house. You said you wouldn't."

"I've had a bad day."

Elaina dug her fingernails into her palms. "We all have bad days."

"When I'm weak, I smoke."

Maybe Arden was right – she had gone insane. She was allowing dog hair, women who pushed her to the edge, and now cigarette smoke. She groaned. If Tawny wanted to smoke, it was her deal, but no way was she going to do it in the house. The smoke messed with her sinuses plus it weaved into the curtains and attached to the paint. "I know. I know. Old habits die hard."

Tawny flinched from the sarcasm.

Livid, Elaina stormed from the bedroom and vibrated the door with a slam. *Stony.* Crap. Stomping back, she stuck her head in the room, trying not to inhale. "Where's Stony?"

Tawny cast her head down and pointed to the small attached bathroom.

"You subjected the love of your life to second-hand smoke? That's messed up."

"I cracked the bathroom window for him."

Elaina turned the knob on the door and Stony loped out.

"I'm sorry, Elaina."

"Yeah. Yeah."

Before she made it to the stairway, Tawny called out in a weepy voice. "I need you. Please don't go."

All Elaina wanted was to escape the real world with a chick flick to even out the frayed edges of her nerves. What she was getting instead was a bigger dose of the real world. Still brimming with anger, she was tempted to keep going. A tiny voice inside warned not to turn her back on the brown-haired smokestack. Returning to Tawny, she forced away the scowl. "I'm not going to lecture you. You know you screwed up."

Tawny's eyes were soulful and watery. "I *really* messed up. Not just with cigarettes."

Elaina emitted another noiseless groan. Despite the air conditioning working at full boost to counter the relentless heat-wave, she opened the window wide. "Let's go to my room while yours airs out."

When they were both tucked in the room across the hall, Elaina sat in the chair by the window and motioned for Tawny to take the other one. A small lamp table sat between them. "Something go awry at the hospital?"

Tawny rubbed a hand back and forth across her

forehead. "Not at work, thank God. But something went horribly awry *after* work."

Elaina didn't recall seeing Tawny's car outside. Then again, she hadn't been looking for it. "Did you get into a wreck?"

Tawny's lashes closed over her eyes, "Ferdinand's fine." The hand that had been on her forehead moved to her belly. "I've puffed away an entire pack of cigarettes in just over an hour and now I'm queasy."

First, Steph. Now, Tawny. Was there a full moon? "You got a speeding ticket?"

"Worse!"

Elaina's fragile control was slipping. "Do I have to keep guessing?"

Tawny buried her face in her hands. "I slept with Grady."

"Whaaaaat?"

"I know. I can't believe it either."

Elaina hadn't seen that coming. "Are you getting back together?"

Tawny removed her hands and vigorously shook her head. "Not in this lifetime. I'm not sure how it happened. I mean, I know how it happened. I went to see him about getting my bicycle. I'd forgotten about it until today. As soon as I was in the house – to beg for it..." A nervous giggle erupted. "For the bike, not sex, Grady offered me a cup of coffee. One thing led to another and we ended up in bed." She shuddered. "Costly mistake. I returned home with no bike and no dignity."

"All that talk at the Chinese restaurant about missing

sex must've taken root in your subconscious."

"Couldn't my brain have led me to Carter Payne instead of my ex?"

"The mind is a peculiar thing. So is the body. Unfortunately, they seldom work together. Instead of pursuing the unknown with Carter, your need for fulfillment took you to familiar territory."

Tawny appeared to sift through the information. "It's bat-crap crazy to fall into bed with someone you despise."

Elaina left the chair to wrap an arm around Tawny. "Don't beat yourself up. You could do worse things than sleep with your ex."

"Like what?"

"Forget to clip your toe nails. Give Stony too many treats. Wash your lingerie with something red. Eat too many bon-bons. The list is endless."

Tawny let go of a genuine laugh. "Thanks for putting your special spin on things, and for making me laugh when I was sure I never would again." She lifted her bare feet. "These toe nails are on the fringe of being a catastrophe. Look how long they're getting."

"They are looking pretty gruesome." Elaina grinned. "I actually came to ask if you'd like to go the theater, but I've changed my mind. I'd rather go for a swim. Join me?" She glanced out the window. The sun was still up, but joined by the moon – which was currently white in the blue sky. And damn if it wasn't full!

"I'm there."

"Wine will be involved."

"Thank goodness."

"We'll drink to tucking away old habits."

"And to making a few new ones that involve phoning a dear friend when I'm about to fall into bed with the wrong guy."

"Amen to that." Elaina couldn't resist. "So how was it?"

"You're getting dunked in the pool."

"You have to catch me first."

"Oh, I'll catch you."

"Are you sure you have the lung capacity?" Elaina pretended to take a puff of a cigarette and dashed down the stairs.

Chapter Sixteen

~ The More the Merrier ~

Breaking the surface of the pool water, Elaina spit and sputtered. "You got me back. Okay? Dunking me five times was plenty. No need for another sneak attack." She chopped the water, cascading it over Tawny.

"That'll teach you to lip off." The mirth vanished and was replaced with big eyes when she looked past Elaina.

Swinging around, Elaina discovered the source of Tawny's surprise. On the patio stood two tall, strapping guys wearing tank tops, khaki shorts, and dark sunglasses. Both had closely cropped hair and face stubble that women – even her age – found sexy.

"Bo! Quentin!" Instead of swimming to get to them, Tawny trekked hard against the waves. "Oh my gosh! It's so good to see you. I didn't think you were coming home until Labor Day weekend." Her voice cracked with emotion. "What are you doing here?"

"Duh," said the taller of the two. "It's your birthday tomorrow. We weren't going to just drop a card in the mail."

"This is such a surprise!"

Bo helped his mom from the pool and Quentin handed her a towel.

"Elaina! My boys!"

Tawny's excitement spilled over to Elaina. She grinned from ear to ear. "Hey, guys." She stayed where she was to give them a few moments of uninterrupted reunion.

They waved but their focus was their mom. Bo hugged Tawny tight and planted a series of kisses across her forehead. Quentin gave her a powerful squeeze and smashed his lips against her cheek.

"Is it safe to come out?" Steph asked from the kitchen.

"Get your butts out here and meet my boys."

Elaina climbed from the pool and made a beeline to the chaise for her beach towel and flip flops. Wrapping the towel around her in the name of modesty, she joined the others. "You just brightened your mother's day."

Bo ran his gaze over Elaina. "You just brightened mine."

Tawny poked him in the ribs. "No lusting on my bestie." As if she thought Steph and Grace would take offense, she added, "Or my other two besties." She introduced all three.

"Tomorrow's your birthday? You conveniently didn't mention it, you sly little fox." Elaina met Tawny's eyes and another piece of the puzzle fell into place. Tawn' sleeping with her ex and smoking like a chimney might've been prompted by the brutal reality of adding another birthday. Being in your forties was empowering in some ways and frightening as hell in others.

"I wanted to turn forty-seven without a lot of hoopla."

"I completely understand."

"You do?" Quentin asked. "I sure don't."

Tawny patted his shoulder. "That's because you're twenty-one. When you're my age you'll try to hide from birthdays."

Quentin rolled his eyes. "Whatever." He picked his mom up, swung her around, and effortlessly tossed her in the pool.

Bo eyed Elaina.

Squinting, she took a step back. "Don't even think about it."

Eyes the color of his mom's, with the same ornery glint, warned it *was* going to happen. In one fluid move, Elaina was wrenched tightly in his arms and they were in the pool before she could protest.

Elaina dunked him several times and splashed for good measure. Laughter pumped from his chest. "Behave, Bo Westerfield." She swam away, glancing over her shoulder to make sure he wasn't after her.

Grace came to the rescue with a stack of dry towels.

"Seriously, Bo, pick on someone your own…" Tawny quirked an eyebrow and left the comment unfinished.

Elaina completed the thought. "Yeah, ya bully. Pick on someone your own…size." She laughed. "Quit giving me the eye. I'm old enough to be your…aunt."

"Why are all the hot chicks old enough to be my aunt?" Bo mocked with a huge grin.

"You'd better watch this one, Tawn'. He's too smooth for his britches."

"Tell me about it. The girls in California don't stand a chance with Bo Westerfield living amongst them." Tawny didn't cloak Bo with all the praise and teasing. She draped some love over Quentin too. "The mothers in Oregon better be on their guard with Quentin within kissing distance of their daughters."

Bo looked remarkably like Tawny. Quentin took after Grady. They both had their mom's easy-going, teasing personality.

While they were frolicking in the pool, Steph made a trip to the kitchen for wine coolers and cans of beer.

Grace did a "Yee-haw" and placed a bounty of pita chips, hummus, and an assortment of fresh veggies on the patio table.

Yee-haw must've meant come-and-get-it in guy language. Bo and Quentin left Tawny and Elaina to grab a beer.

"Carrots and celery?" Bo made a face but adjusted it to a cocky grin. "It makes sense. Mom says you're the fitness queen of Cherry Ridge."

"Damn skippy, I am." Elaina crunched on a carrot stick.

"Just be glad there isn't broccoli on the plate." Steph pulled the strings off a stick of celery.

"Give it to me straight, Quentin. Why did you and Bo hop a plane home? I'm tickled you're here but there's more to it than my birthday."

Quentin's gaze zipped to Bo. "We haven't been home in a while."

"Aaaaand?"

Bo's expression gave little away.

"We decided to see for ourselves what was happening in your world. You said you were fine. Dad said you were fine. All that *fineness* felt contrived."

Bo shoulder-bumped his mom. "I guess we worried for nothing. You seem happy."

"I am happy." Tawny looked from Elaina to Steph and then to Grace. "Moving in here was a good decision. These ladies keep me on my toes. They're fun and fearless. When life bogs me down, they pull me up. They're not afraid to tell me if I get out of line. Best of all, they love Stony."

Bo's brown eyes sparkled. "Stony's here?"

"He's inside keeping cool."

"Shared-custody?"

"Did your Dad fail to mention he gave me Stony?"

"He didn't say a word. Then again, he let on that everything was *fine*."

"Everything *is* fine, Bo."

"Quentin and I were at Dad's for maybe five minutes. I can't believe I didn't ask about Stony."

Elaina was stunned when Bo enveloped her in a hug, instead of his mom.

"You rock. Letting my mom *and* Stony move in is beyond generous." He flashed a pearly-white smile at Tawny. "Mom would be lost without him."

Elaina put a hand on his chest and moved him back. "They're both awesome."

Grace uncapped a raspberry wine cooler. "We've all fallen for the dog. One look in those blue eyes and we were goners."

"The ladies say that about my eyes too." Bo snagged a handful of carrots from the plate.

"Oh barf," Quentin said.

Elaina shivered from the dampness of her swim suit. "I'm heading in to change."

"We wanted to surprise you, Mom." Quentin kissed Tawny's temple. "But we should probably head back to Dad's place." He crunched a pita chip. "We'll catch up with you tomorrow. Can we take you out to lunch?"

"Would it be uncomfortable if we brought Dad along?" Bo asked.

Tawny tried to appear unaffected, but Elaina saw a blaze of 'hell yes it would be uncomfortable' in her eyes.

Grace, God love her, came up with a compromise. "If you're bringing him, we're also coming."

Tawny seemed relieved. "I don't go anywhere without my peeps."

"Peeps?" Elaina said to mock.

Quentin studied his mom. "The more the merrier."

* * *

Steph whispered behind her hand. "Aaaawkward."

"Understatement," Elaina replied without moving her lips.

Tawny took a spot at the end of the table. Grady had command of the opposite end. The only reassuring thing about the whole setup was if a food fight took place it would be long way for them to hurl dinner rolls at each other.

While the waitress handed out menus, Elaina assessed the situation. Tawny and Grady had been civil thus far. Neither one had said 'bite me' or 'kiss my rump', nor had they stuck a foot out to trip the other. Still, Tawny was clearly under stress. She'd been chewing her nails; some of which had to be down to the quick. Her posture was rod straight and her mouth was a thin, grim line; not exactly the look of someone celebrating a birthday. Grady, on the other hand, wore a smirk the size of Ohio. Elaina wished she would've sat closer to *accidentally* kick his shins if he got out of line.

Lost in thought, Grace tapped her shoulder. "Your turn."

Elaina folded her menu. "I'll have a Chef salad. No dressing."

Grace snickered. "We're not ordering food yet, just drinks."

Elaina blinked up at the waitress. "Something red, sweet, and potent. Moscato?"

The waitress nodded. "A bottle or glass?"

"Three bottles and seven glasses."

Grady shot his mouth off. "I'm not paying for three bottles of wine."

Tawny leveled a hard stare at her ex.

Bo took the limelight. "Parents. Whatcha gonna do?"

Elaina waved a hand. "No worries. I've got it." She smiled at the waitress. "Put everything on one check."

Bo and Quentin balked. Grady seemed satisfied. Tawny looked like she wanted to stab him with her fork.

"We'll also need a cake." Elaina looked at Tawny.

"Chocolate?"

"Yes. Please."

"No candles though," Steph interjected. "Forty-seven of those bad boys would burn the place down."

Finally, a 'bite me' from Tawny.

Everyone laughed, including the waitress.

"Oh my gosh, Wendy. It's the fun ladies." A voice Elaina had heard before sounded from behind.

She swiveled around to recognize Melanie, their waitress from the steakhouse. "Obviously we made an impression."

Melanie's smile was infectious. "I remember lots of wine and talking about guys with long…" She clamped her mouth shut.

Elaina thought the abrupt cut in conversation was because Melanie discovered they weren't alone. That was partly true. Mel and Bo were both glassy-eyed and boring a hole through each other.

Steph nudged Elaina with her elbow. "Love is in the air."

Wendy broke the trance by waving a hand in front of Melanie's face. "We should let these folks order."

Bo was out of his chair at lightning speed. "Eat with us." He grabbed two chairs from a nearby table. He ordered Quentin out of the way to make room for the cute arrivals. As though he remembered Elaina was footing the bill, he sought her out. "Is it okay?"

"It's okay with me, but you really should ask your mom. It's her birthday." Elaina was fascinated at how her small world had grown. A few weeks ago it was 'Samuels, party of one'. Today, it was party of nine.

Bo's gaze skipped to his mom and he put his hand on his chest. "Don't break my heart, Tawny. Say yes."

Tawny lifted an authoritative eyebrow. "The name's Mom." She grinned at Melanie. "Be warned. This might seem like one of those easy-peasy join-us moments, but it's so much more. Bo has stars in his eyes and he's puffing out his chest."

"Sweet. Me too." Melanie parked beside Bo and Wendy took a seat next to Quentin.

Steph whispered to Grace but Elaina overhead. "Should we make them honorary members of the wine club?"

Grace didn't pause to think it over. "They could probably teach us a thing or two, but I'm taking the snob route and voting no. More isn't always merrier. Sometimes it's just more."

Steph's forehead crinkled.

"In other words, I need the comfort of those who understand the idea of been-there done-that."

The lines in Steph's forehead deepened; evidence she still didn't get it.

"Sheesh. I should've brought an Etch-A-Sketch along to draw you a picture." Grace sounded annoyed. She shifted in her seat and tried again. "I need to be surrounded by women my age; not by those who think a bucket list is something they keep at a home improvement store."

Awareness flashed across Steph's expression. Defiance flashed across her words. "I still vote yes."

Elaina pretended not to have heard. She wanted to remain neutral but the little gremlin in her brain kicked her left hemisphere with a reality check. It would be difficult to remain nonaligned. At some point, one of her friends would draw her in with a good argument. The one regarding Melanie and Wendy, however, wasn't a real issue. For now, the wine club would remain at four members.

Chapter Seventeen

~ *Say What?* ~

Stony had been keeping his distance most of the day. Elaina thought it odd, but then, dogs were allowed to have their moods just like people. She walked by him, ran her fingers across his head and down his back. "Everything okay, boy?"

He lowered his head to the floor.

Elaina crouched beside him. Stony was usually putty in her hands when she petted him. He'd roll to his back so she could also give his belly some attention. Not this time, however. He didn't try to lick her and he made a weird noise, deep in his throat. "Did Quentin feed you too many cheese puffs?" After lunch, everyone except for Grady had come back to the house for a swim and small talk. Grace had prepared a plate of sea salt crackers, pepper jack and Muenster cheeses, and red seedless grapes. Quentin had brought a case of Bud Light and a family-size bag of cheese puffs. It didn't take an Einstein to figure out Stony had been slipped a few of the puffs. His whiskers had been coated with orange. "Hang in there, babe. It'll pass."

Bo, Quentin, Mel, and Wendy were long gone. Everyone else had headed to their bedrooms but Elaina wasn't sleepy. She removed her iPad from the charger. Intending to relax in the recliner with a spicy romance, she performed the nightly ritual of flicking off lights and securing the door locks. She made her way down the short, dimly lit hallway to the back door, cheerily humming *All Summer Long* by Kid Rock. Her foot slipped in something warm and squishy. Reeling out of control while screeching, she thudded against the steel door.

Elaina reached for the light switch to verify what she already knew; Stony had gotten sick. Revulsion leapt in her throat. She hopped on one foot to the half-bath off the kitchen, vowing to throttle Quentin if she got a chance.

Gone was her good mood. She was tempted to wake Tawny to make her deal with the mess. Instead, she donned a pair of rubber gloves, grabbed a roll of paper towels, and a spray bottle of disinfectant.

"It's midnight and I'm cleaning orange dog vomit." She cussed and went at the mess with a vengeance.

With the hallway sanitized, she went in search of Stony who was no longer lying near his water bowl. The poor thing might not have understood her words, but no doubt he picked up on her anger. Now he was in hiding.

"Stony," she called in a low voice. Dogs were supposed to have a great sense of hearing. He didn't come running.

Elaina tried again. "Come here, sweet boy. I'm not

mad…at you." Still, no sign of him. She checked behind the sofa. Big blue eyes stared up at her. Dropping to her knees, she resorted to baby talk. "It's not your fault. Those cheese puffs gave you a bellyache. Would you like to go for a walk? It'll make you feel better." She tugged at his collar.

Stony reluctantly left the safety of the sofa.

Grabbing the leash from the hook in the hallway, she wiggled her toes into Tawny's flip flops.

The moon was mostly full, illuminating the dark sky, making it seem like early evening instead of minutes into the new day. A warm breeze swept across her as she led the hairy pooch down the sidewalk.

No longer angry, Elaina marveled at the fact she was traipsing around the neighborhood in the dark of night. It was refreshing. Liberating. Weird. In a way, those feelings described more than just the moment. They also depicted how her life was shaping up post-divorce. She could thank Tawny, Steph, and Grace for that. Meeting them had been a godsend. "You, Stone-man, are the glue that makes this crazy set of circumstances stick." She bent down and planted a kiss on his head. "Do you want to go around the block or go home?" He blinked, nothing more.

"Good one, Samuels. You're expecting him to answer like he's Scooby Doo."

After walking around the large city block, she decided to keep going. One block led to another. Before she realized it, she'd made it downtown. The clock on St. Joseph's Catholic Church struck one o'clock. "We should probably head back."

Stony had other ideas and tugged in the opposite direction.

"Yeah, I don't want to go home either."

At two-thirty, Elaina got spooked by the sound of metal trash cans being knocked over. All kinds of scenarios rushed through her head. Cherry Ridge wasn't the crime capital of Ohio, but it was known to have a few troublemakers. If someone was up to no good, she needed to get out of their way.

Speed-walking in flip-flops, she and Stony made the trek back home in record time. Twisting the doorknob, nothing happened. "What the…?" Since she didn't bring a key, she'd made sure the door was left ajar. It was now locked. She rang the doorbell. When no one showed up to let her in, she rang it again. "One of you should hear the ding-dong." In hindsight, she should've taken her key, set the security alarm, and locked the door. With four women coming and going at all hours, she'd gotten lax with the alarm. Lesson learned.

Except for the hoot of an owl in the far distance, there was complete silence.

Trudging to the front door, Elaina laid on the doorbell.

A beam of light from an approaching car hit Elaina in the eyes.

The car slowed and came to a stop in front of the house.

The reflective emblem on the passenger door was a welcome sight. "Help has arrived."

Two uniformed officers stepped from the car with

their hands touching their holstered weapons.

The hair on the back of Elaina's neck prickled.

"Ma'am," the lead officer said, "I'm going to ask you to step away from the door."

"Come again?"

"Step. Away. From. The. Door."

The authority in the man's tenor made Elaina flinch. "I live here. I locked myself out."

He pointed to the sidewalk. "Until we verify the accuracy of that claim you need to remove yourself from the porch."

"Would I try to break into a residence with a dog in hand?"

Again, the officer pointed.

Elaina didn't relish the thought of being tazered. She grudgingly obeyed.

The second officer walked to the door and knocked instead of ringing the bell.

Elaina was tempted to say, "Good luck with that."

A light in the living room came on.

"Are you kidding me?"

The front door opened and Steph stood holding her robe closed.

"Good evening, miss. We've identified the source of your concern." The officer shined his long handled flashlight at Elaina.

Steph's eyes went wide. "Oops. There's been a mistake. She lives here. Actually, this is her house."

"Ohhh," the officer drew out. He glanced at Elaina. "I'm sorry I couldn't take your word for it."

"You scared the bejesus out of me when you put your hands on your guns."

The corners of the officers' mouth started to turn up but he staved off the smile before it happened.

Steph snickered. "At least they didn't handcuff you."

Elaina frowned. "I'm glad one of us finds this funny."

"You will too. In the morning."

Tawny pushed her way beside Steph. "I told her it was silly to call 9-1-1. We heard a scream followed by a thump. When we couldn't find you we thought the worst. There were no signs of a struggle but criminals don't always leave a mess."

No, but sick dogs do. "I took Stony for a walk." Elaina wanted to say more but she wouldn't go into a lengthy explanation with the officers present.

Grace shoved her way between Tawny and Steph. "Officer, you should probably frisk her."

The officer didn't play along. "We'll let you ladies sort this out. Have a good evening."

Elaina held out her wrists. "I'll save you a return trip. Go ahead and cuff me because once I get inside I'm going to wring their necks."

* * *

"I'm paying big bucks for my membership but I'm not losing weight."

Yeah? Well I want a bubble bath and glass of wine. Elaina was too tired to deal with Hazel Montpelier who was standing with her feet shoulder-width apart, hands on her hips, and a cutting glare deep enough to cause permanent wrinkles. "Can we discuss this in private?" Elaina asked.

Hazel's voice notched higher. "No we cannot! We're going to talk about this right here, right now."

Fatigued from lack of sleep thanks to last night's circus, Elaina's patience was hanging by a flimsy string. "Go ahead and air your grievances," she said wryly.

"I just did! Weren't you listening?"

"I heard the bit about not losing weight but there's always more to the story. Along with your exercise regimen, have you altered your eating habits?"

"So it's MY fault!"

It was hard to remain professional with missiles of hostility being fired. "That's not what I said." Elaina walked behind the counter and clicked into the membership roster. She located Hazel's account. "According to my records you've only been here four times this month. When you joined I suggested you exercise at least three times a week."

Hazel dodged the facts. "With the chores I do at home, combined with what I do here, ten pounds should've melted away. I'VE GAINED FIVE!"

Holding back a yawn, Elaina didn't allow the woman's anxiety to get to her. Lethargic and in no mood to argue, she informed Hazel she would reimburse the full price of her membership.

Michael Rexx walked by with mischief dancing in his eyes. "I wouldn't give her a dime." He'd obviously heard the conversation and was trying to ease the tension.

Elaina didn't know what to make of Michael. He was a big dose of charm and a constant flirt. Part of her wanted to pounce on him with a lusty kiss. The other part wanted to place more pylons around her for protection. She watched him walk to the stretching area before she returned her attention to the angry woman.

Hazel's taut expression had surprisingly lessened and the antagonism was nearly gone from her tone. "I don't want to quit my membership." Her brown eyes watered. "I want to get the flab off." Inhaling a strong breath, she blew it out before divulging the real reason behind her dissatisfaction. "My husband's losing interest in me."

You could've knocked Elaina over with a mere flick. Gym owners, like bartenders, were occasionally the recipients of too-much-information. "Oh Hazel," she said softly, "let's talk about this in there." She pointed to the private room.

Hazel's shoulders drooped. "I didn't mean to bite your head off. It was a transference thing. My husband bit mine off and I did the same to you."

Inside the small room, Elaina sat on the padded window seat. Hazel did the same.

Before Elaina could offer empathy, Hazel burst into tears. "John's made it clear that my body doesn't do anything for him anymore. He called me a train-wreck. What am I going to do?"

Elaina impulsively pulled Hazel into an embrace. She wanted to say something profound and reassuring, but what? Her own marriage had hit a pile of rocks. If Hazel's husband was so bold and hurtful to tell his wife she didn't turn him on anymore, Hazel needed to speak with a relationship expert not the owner of a gym. "I can offer a plan of attack regarding your weight and an ear to listen. Beyond that I'm clueless."

"I know you can't fix what's going on but you're my starting point." She grabbed hold of the jelly roll around her middle. "Help me with this. If you can design a plan of attack, I'll welcome it. My challenge will be to figure out how I can fit it in though, with everything else I have to do. The day job sucks the life out of me and I have little left for the kids, housekeeping, and trying to please John. Some days I want to cover my head with the blankets and stay in bed because I don't have anything to give." Tears tracked down her cheeks.

Elaina handed Hazel a box of tissues. "If men were forced to do what we do for one day, they'd be more understanding. Aaaand...they'd be exhausted by noon."

"You're right."

"This might come off as a programmed sales pitch, but getting into a structured exercise routine will increase your energy level. I can't guarantee it will hop you up like an 'energy' drink, but it'll put some oomph in your step."

"I need some oomph and a few body tucks. Three pregnancies have rearranged everything." Putting her hands high on her chest, Hazel winced. "My boobs used to be up here. Now they're headed to my waist. My tush is just as saggy."

Hazel was trying to be super-woman but the costume with the big S on the front no longer fit. Elaina spoke soothingly. "First and foremost, you need to look in the mirror to appreciate the beautiful woman who gave birth to three little miracles." Emotion welled up inside of Elaina. "You're a strong person, Hazel. You have to be to handle everything on your plate. But in order to achieve a slim, tight body, you have to alter your way of thinking. If you want to lose weight," she leaned to tap Hazel's temple, "it starts here. Tell yourself you can do it. You'll increase your chances of success if you do this for you, not for someone else."

Hazel blew her nose. "I get what you're saying."

Elaina heard a 'but' even though Hazel didn't utter it.

Hazel's cell phone chimed from her pocket. "I have to take this."

"No worries." Elaina stepped from the room to give Hazel privacy to field the call and to give her a few moments for things to sink in.

She'd just stepped behind the counter when Michael returned.

"Everything okay?"

"Everything's fine." Nothing was fine. She was tired, cranky, and wishing it was nine o'clock so she could shoo everyone out.

"You look like you could use a naked massage."

Elaina's jaw dropped. "Say what?"

"You heard me. We could both use some naked time. You in?"

Chapter Eighteen

- It Ain't Gonna Happen -

"I know I'm going to regret declining your invitation but I'm not ready to take my clothes off."

"New offer. Dinner. Drinks. Fully-clothed massage."

Elaina smiled half-heartedly. "I'd be lousy company." She wasn't just making an excuse to dodge a romp with Michael. She really was in a funk.

Michael's gaze combed over her with curiosity. "Did the member with less-than-stellar weight loss upset you?"

"No. She and I are okay. What started out as a blow-up turned into something quite different."

"Good to hear." He leaned across the counter to make the space between them more personal. "Is it me? Am I coming on too strong? Are you hell-bent on holding onto the guideline? Does the idea of getting naked with me scare you?"

The questions were complicated but she didn't have to dig deep for the answers. She already knew she liked Michael. He was appealing, and unusual, in a good way. His straightforward-without-being-pushy approach kept her from telling him to jump off a cliff. If she had to pick one thing she liked about him, other than his amazing eyes, it would be his sense of humor. He didn't make her roll with laughter but his dry wit made her chuckle. So no, he wasn't coming on too strong. She was flattered he was still hot on her trail even though she wasn't dropping many breadcrumbs for him to follow. "The idea of getting naked with *anyone* sends panic rushing through my bloodstream."

Michael's voice turned gooey and warm like melted caramel. "It's not just me but the entire male species?"

It was rhetorical so Elaina didn't feel the need to answer.

"After my world fell apart I vowed to keep women at bay." One bushy eyebrow lifted and his mouth inclined into a goofy grin. "Since I'm not into guys I had to modify my stance. Plus, there's one spectacular woman who adjusted my way of thinking the moment I laid eyes on her." Michael tugged a leather cardholder from his shirt pocket. Handing her one of his business cards, his fingers made contact.

Elaina flinched at the unexpected tingles furiously tracking up her arm. She was even more shocked by the bursts of pleasure that followed. Nothing so strange… and incredible…had ever happened quite like it; not even with the man who had her heart for more years than she cared to remember. Bunching her face in bewilderment, she read the card aloud to distract the odd enjoyment. "Michael Rexx – independent trucker. No job too big or too small. Call for estimates." Flipping the card several times, she met his eyes. "I need to call you for an estimate when I'm ready to get naked?"

"Duh," he teased.

"If you're too expensive I might have to go elsewhere." Elaina's chest bounced with a laugh but the thought of being naked in Michael's arms was no laughing matter. In fact, there was absolutely no mirth involved; just a ton of uncertainty and an equal amount of fear. If and when she was ready to be with a man again without a stitch on, she hoped it would be with him. Until then, the protective pylons would remain in place.

Michael was still stretched across the counter. "I should quit picturing you sans clothes." He glanced back to the workout area. "Everyone in the place will know. If you get my drift."

"I get your drift." Elaina pressed her lips together.

Michael swallowed hard and his Adam's apple bobbed. "The imagination is a powerful thing." He cleared his throat. "Back to my original inquiry. What's bugging you?"

Elaina tucked the card in her purse. "You don't want to hear the things going on in my head."

"Yes I do."

The sincerity in his voice made Elaina's heart scrunch. She wasn't used to this kind of consideration. Arden had never been one to listen. Suck-it-up and self-soothe had been his motto. Pfft. The longer she was away from the barracuda the more she realized he'd never been her soul mate. Elaina stared into the eyes of the guy who was desperately trying to fill the position. Before she could think things through, she shared too much. "I've been second-guessing some recent decisions."

"Does it have to do with letting Grace, Steph, and Tawny move in?"

Was she that easy to read? Running her fingers over her eyebrow, she pondered the wisdom of spilling her guts. Revealing that Steph, Tawny, and Grace were indeed driving her bonkers would be the same as stabbing them in the back. At the same time, she was fast becoming an active volcano. If she didn't tell someone what was going on, lava would spew and it wouldn't be pretty.

"Lower your fences," he said quietly.

In a way, it would be easier to take off her clothes for the naked massage, than it would be to divulge her secrets.

Michael brought his watch into view. "When do you get off work?"

"In fifteen minutes."

"We could go to my place. Over coffee and a sandwich you can confirm I was right and I can help you figure things out."

"Or I could go home, take a hot bath, and have a glass of Merlot."

Michael smiled but there was a periphery of hurt in his eyes. "You can't blame a guy for trying."

* * *

Elaina had driven around Cherry Ridge until she'd been on every street twice. Earlier, she'd sent her housemates a text stating she wouldn't get home until late. She asked them not to call the cops if they heard someone rattling the back door. Steph responded with 'Good one'. Grace's reply came as an LOL. Tawny said she had the cops on speed dial. None of them asked where she was or what she was doing. Good thing. She didn't want to fib. And she certainly didn't want to tell the truth.

The digital numbers on the dash said she should head for home, or possibly risk another encounter with Cherry Ridge's finest.

Putting down the street at a grand five miles an hour, Elaina removed her foot from the accelerator and coasted. When a car came from the opposite direction, she sped up so they wouldn't think she was casing the neighborhood.

Her two story house came into view. Instead of pulling into the driveway, she kept going. "Get a grip." Elaina put the car in reverse and backed into the drive. She waited until the light flicked off in Tawny's bedroom before she climbed from the SUV.

On the way to the house, she took a deep breath. Keeping her distance from the women she'd grown fond of was silly. It didn't fix what was wrong, just delayed the conflict. Really, there wasn't one thing in particular she could address if she confronted them. It was a bunch of little things driving her bananas.

Looking over her shoulder for reflective police emblems, Elaina shoved the key in the lock.

The second she stepped inside, Stony greeted her with a heartwarming yowl.

"Shh." Bending down, she petted his furry head and stroked his back. "We don't want to wake everyone." She thought it peculiar that he wasn't upstairs lying on the floor beside Tawny. Maybe his belly was misbehaving again. She checked the floor for evidence. There were no signs he was sick. Then it struck her that he might've been waiting for her to come home. "I love you, Stony."

Tossing her purse and keys on the counter, she dug in the plastic tote for a treat. Kissing him just above the eyes, she whispered. "Time to pee."

Stony looked up from the goody.

"Not you, me. Too much iced tea." Elaina shuffled to the half-bath.

The sound of the suction being broken on the freezer door indicated someone was up. Elaina went still, hoping whoever it was would get what they came for and head back upstairs.

A minute seemed like ten.

Ten seemed like twenty.

Alrighty then. The late-night-snacker was taking her good old time.

Elaina stepped from the bathroom.

Steph's eyes rounded with surprise and the spoonful of Cherry Garcia stopped short of her mouth. "What are you doing?"

"I could ask you the same question." Elaina eyed the carton of decadent dessert.

Steph clanged the spoon into the sink. "Don't judge me."

Elaina snickered but afterward wished she hadn't.

"I'm not judging you."

"I see it in your eyes."

"Where is this coming from, Steph?"

Shoving the carton of ice cream into the freezer with the lid cockeyed, Steph glared. "My life sucks."

Elaina closed the distance between them and put a hand on Steph's shoulder.

Steph shrugged away.

"Did you run into Corbett today?"

"This isn't about Corbett," Steph ground out between clenched teeth.

Elaina teetered back at the caustic tone. "Then what? Or who?" Surely she wasn't pissed because they'd heckled her last night about getting a mammogram today. Grace had described the procedure as getting her boobs squished in a vise. Tawny had made a crack about the tech having to find Steph's boobs first before they could be squashed. It had been in good fun but maybe they'd gone too far. "Are you mad because we kidded about your lack of boobs?"

Steph's scowl deepened. She wildly threw her hands up. "I can't do this. None of it. I want to eat myself silly. I want my sweat pants back."

Elaina knew better than to tell her to calm down. Instead, she chose an alternate approach. "We all backslide. It happens. The best remedy is to have a bowl of ice cream and start over tomorrow."

"Start over?" Steph stomped to the freezer and pulled out the Cherry Garcia again. "Start over?" she repeated. "How can I start over when I never actually began?"

"You ate broccoli until you gassed us in the elevator. I've seen you snacking on carrots and celery."

Steph's groan was filled with pain. "I've been shoving candy bars into my mouth at an alarming rate."

"You said you lost weight."

Steph didn't come right out and say she lied, but her guilty look said as much.

Elaina tried to move in again, only to be straight-armed. "I don't understand."

"You're in the business of fitness but you don't understand. Well that's rich."

"I'm not a psychologist."

"Yet you have no problem telling me what I should and shouldn't do."

Elaina allowed the meanness spewing from Steph to hurt her feelings. "You asked for guidance. I thought that's what I was giving you."

Steph pushed ice cream into her mouth and licked the spoon clean. "I know how to eat, what to eat, how much to eat. All I needed was encouragement."

Elaina went from being hurt to seeing red. "I'm trying to keep my cool but you keep poking me with a stick." She wanted to say a hell of a lot more. Instead, she fled up the stairs.

"Yeah that's it. Take your slim figure up those stairs," Steph said vehemently.

Elaina stopped three steps short of the top. "Until you identify what's really *eating* at you, food is going to anchor you down – in more ways than one. I'll be the fall-girl if you need someone to blame. But you and I both know, when you point a finger, there's four more pointing back at you. The smokin' hot body you wanted isn't going to happen until you discover you're worth it."

Chapter Nineteen

~ *More Than Monkeys, It Would Seem* ~

The kitchen phone ringing off the hook perked up Elaina more than the coffee she'd intentionally made extra strong. "Hello."

"Hey, it's Cody Cordray. Is my mom around? I called her cell phone three times and she's not answering."

"I'm not completely sure, but I think she's in the shower, Cody."

"I have to leave for work in fifteen minutes. Is there any chance you could take the phone to her?"

"For some reason the darn thing cuts out when I take it upstairs. I'm going to lay it down and have her come to you."

"Sounds like a plan. Thanks."

"You're welcome." Elaina hurried upstairs, hollering for Grace.

Grace stepped from her room with a towel-turban around her head. "You summoned?"

"Your son's on the phone. He tried your cell."

Grace held up her phone. "I saw I had three missed

calls. I've tried to call him but his phone keeps going to voice mail."

"It's because he's tied up on the phone downstairs. Let's go."

When they got to the kitchen, the phone was back in the cradle. Elaina went into a panic. "Why isn't the phone still on the counter?"

Tawny opened the newspaper and nonchalantly spread it out on the table. "I thought you forgot to put it back."

"Tawn', Grace's boy was on hold."

"Eep. Sorry."

"He was calling from Italy!" Fat tears flooded Grace's eyes; some rolled down her cheeks. Still clutching her cell she entered Cody's number, leaving the tears unattended.

Tawny appeared stunned. "Is she hormonal?"

The old adage about the straw that broke the camel's back fit the moment. Elaina fisted her hands. *Just breathe. Just breathe.*

"He's not answering," Grace said in a broken voice.

"Chill. He's probably texting his friends. You know how kids are." Tawny flipped to the next page in the newspaper.

Grace dropped her face into her hands.

"Don't tell her to chill." Elaina frowned. "Grace isn't hormonal. She needed a kid-fix. You of all people should understand."

"Somebody got up on the wrong side of bed."

Elaina trembled with anger. She huffed out a breath like a bull snorting. "Unbelievable." She brusquely grabbed her purse.

Tawny still appeared to have no clue. "Can you follow me to the car dealership? I'm getting Ferdinand's oil changed and his tires rotated."

"The only place I'm going to is Lake Erie." Her voice boomed louder with each word. "I've made a split-second decision to take the break I mentioned a while back."

"Fabulous," Tawny said dryly. "Grace is bawling. You're bitching. Steph blew out of here a minute ago, looking like she could bite the head off a bat."

"Exactly."

"Exactly what?"

* * *

Elaina sat on the balcony of the small Cape Cod rental overlooking glorious Lake Erie with her iPad reading Gone Girl by Gillian Flynn. This was the life. Peace and quiet. No monkeys. No circus. Just seagulls and sunshine. Laying her feet on a padded wicker ottoman, she sipped Pinot Noir from a wine glass etched with gold leaves. "Gillian, you literary minx. You have me on the edge of my seat." Swiping her finger across the iPad she moved to the next chapter. She was so caught up in the story that when The Ohio State fight-song blasted from her phone, she almost knocked over the wine glass. "Nope. Not answering. When I said I was taking a break, I meant it." Curiosity made her lean to identify the caller. Stephanie Mathews displayed on the face of the phone. Elaina wasn't holding a grudge, but her feelings were still raw. "Whatever you have to say can wait." She turned the volume down to the lowest setting. Changing her mind, she put the phone on vibrate.

Going back to the thriller layered with suspense and filled with twisting plots, Elaina was held captive until the riot of thoughts she'd pushed out, found their way back in. She shifted restlessly until she'd dragged herself out of the chair. Leaning against the railing, she watched the ferry service take another load of folks over to Put-in-Bay.

Her phone had the audacity to chime with a voice mail. "You're trying my patience."

Elaina laced her fingers and stretched them over her head for a full body stretch. What she needed to get her mojo back was a runners-high. Earlier she'd seen two guys running on Water Street and considered doing the same, but she'd chosen to relax instead. Now running seemed like a great idea.

Stepping inside, she donned a neon-green tank top for visibility and changed from flip flops to running shoes. To warm her muscles, she jogged in place for ten minutes, then got down on the floor to plank. A lot of runners didn't consider planking, but Elaina knew it would help her run 'tall'. When you got tired, it was a natural thing to bend forward. Strong core muscles prevented that from happening. Next, she engaged in double-leg pelvic tilts to help keep her lower back level when she ran. She did a few squats and a number of hamstring and calf stretches. Mapping her route with the *iMapMyRun* app on her phone, it was time to ramp up the endorphins.

Traffic was sparse and a light breeze blew in off the lake making the June heat easier to handle.

The more she ran, the more she smiled. Pumping her fist, she said, "Yessss." She felt strong, her time was on target, and breathing wasn't a problem.

Fifteen minutes into the run, she made the first turn of the five mile loop onto Schoolhouse Road and almost fell in her tracks when a violent cramp seized her calf. Moaning and limping off the road, she collapsed onto the grass. Elaina grabbed the meaty part of her calf with one hand and placed the other at the top of her Achilles tendon just above the ankle. Pushing her hands together, she assisted her muscles in completing the contraction. It hurt like crazy, but she repeated the process until the charlie horse was gone. Wiping a line of sweat from her forehead, she blamed the cramp on lack of hydration. If she'd been thinking clearly, she would've postponed the run until the wine was mostly out of her system. Therein lay the problem. She hadn't been thinking clearly.

Another plink sounded from her pocket. Prepared to ignore the text message, she continued to work on the tender muscle.

Yet another plink.

"Leave. Me. Alone."

The darn thing continued to plink and Elaina was close to skipping the phone across the asphalt. "All right all ready! You win. If it's something silly, you'll wish you hadn't called."

The first message was from Tawny. *Grace didn't come*

home last night.

"She's a big girl." Elaina tucked the phone away without checking the other messages. "Not my circus. Not my monkeys."

She might've been able to tuck the phone away, but not her thoughts. Did Grace get her fill of the nonsense too? Did she and Tawny have a knock-down drag-out fight after she left? Or did something worse happen? She refused to entertain the last possibility.

"Not my circus."

Her calf went into another spasm. It took a good five minutes, and a slew of cuss words, to get the contraction to settle down.

Sweat ran down Elaina's temples. Hurting, hot, and dying for a glass of water she started the trip back to the rental by walking instead of running. A black cat ran out in front of her. "I knew you'd show up sooner or later." The day Millicent Markward narked out Arden, she'd asked Elaina if a black cat had crossed her path. At the time, the answer had been no. Now it was a solid yes.

The cat didn't cross the road. It zigzagged back and forth. "That can't be good." She passed it but looked over her shoulder. The poor thing was disoriented. Elaina was sure it would get hit by a car if she didn't do something. Braving superstition and the possibility it might be sick, she scooped up the furry creature and took it to the nearest house.

"Is this your cat?"

A guy spraying the soap off a newly washed Malibu adamantly shook his head.

Elaina stopped at the next two houses with the same inquiry and received similar reactions. Crap. "Not my circus. Not my monkeys. Not my cat."

Right.

* * *

Locating an empty cardboard box in the closet, she poked holes in the top. "Temporary housing, my friend."

The cat purred and she was hooked. Dammit. She was now a cat owner. "Let's see, three roomies, one hairy dog, and a sickly looking cat. All I need now is a mouthy parrot."

Placing a small bowl of milk in the box, she tweaked the cat's tail. "Taking you in is probably a huge blunder. One of many. But that's neither here nor there. I'm off to buy cat food and a carrier. On the way, I'm calling the veterinary office to arrange for shots and neutering."

The cat meowed.

"Are you sure you want to hang with me? You've been in my company for a half hour and I'm already talking about having neeldles stuck in you and putting you under the knife. Oh, and the dog I mentioned, he's ten times your size. I'm not sure he'll eat you for a snack, but there's always the possibility. So you have two choices: come home with me to join the rest of us strays, or wander aimlessly around Port Clinton. You don't have to decide now, but I'll need an answer soon." She topped the box with the lid and left at the sound of the cat trying to scratch her way out.

Elaina did the unthinkable – she dialed the home phone.

"It's about time you called," Tawny shrieked.

"Hello to you, too."

Tawny talked a mile a minute. "Grace is nowhere to be found. I checked at the bank and they said she took a day of vacation. I spoke with her niece. She hasn't seen her. Grace won't answer her phone or my text messages. I'm at my wits end."

"She's stonewalling you."

There was a long pause.

"Because I accidentally hung up the phone?"

"I think it's a combination of things."

"Such as?"

Elaina wouldn't catalogue everyone's missteps, at least not over the phone. "This discussion needs to happen in person with all four of us present."

"What did I do so wrong?"

"It's not exclusively about you. It's about all of us. We jumped into this arrangement without thinking things through."

"Are you saying it was a mistake?"

"Not exactly."

"Well that's freaking peachy." Tawny slammed the phone down before Elaina could climb out of the hole she'd dug.

"Good one, Samuels. You said this should be discussed in person yet you hurled a grenade through the phone line." Elaina scrolled through her preprogrammed numbers until she came to Grace. "I might as well throw another one."

Grace picked up right away. "Don't give me a sermon. I know I messed up."

"I won't give you one, if you don't give me one."

"Huh?"

"You and I are doing the same things."

"You've opened the Trojan Pleasure Pack too?"

"Whaaaat?"

"Let the lecturing begin."

It was a pinch-me moment. "Are you saying what I think you're saying?"

Grace started to cry. Not sniffing with an occasional whimper. She engaged in all-out sobbing, complete with hiccups.

Grace's tears took Elaina to the verge of doing the same. "Grace, honey, talk to me."

"I...I...I'm such an idiot!"

Elaina pulled into the Wal-Mart parking lot and turned off the ignition to give her full attention. "Whatever you've done can't be that bad. Unless you kneed your boss in the nads or held up a liquor store." She heard a small, weepy chuckle on the other end.

"You do paint a picture."

"With your bosses junk out of the way, can we move on to why you're upset? I have a good idea what it is, but I want to hear it from you."

"Elaina." There was a long silent gap. "I slept with Dalton James."

Bingo!

The hiccupped-sobs returned.

"Sweetie, it's okay. More than okay. You didn't do anything wrong."

Grace's distress became tortured wails. "I…I tarnished my love for Brince."

Elaina could no longer hold back her own tears. She cried hard, feeling every bit of Grace's pain. Wiping her eyes with the back of her hand, she fumbled in her purse for a tissue. Trying to blow her nose and hold the phone, she almost dropped it. "You didn't desecrate what you and Brince shared. I didn't know Brince, but the fact you hold him in such high regard says he was a great guy. That great guy would want you to be happy. Cody has said as much." A light bulb went off. "Were you able to get a hold of Cody the other day?"

Grace uttered a wobbly, "Yes."

Elaina mulled over a burning question. "I want to ask you something but I'm afraid you'll hang up on me like Tawny did a little bit ago."

"Tawny hung up on you?"

"Slammed the receiver down so hard she probably broke the phone."

"What a hothead."

"Actually, she was going ballistic with worry. I didn't help matters that I shot off my mouth."

"I'm sorry I caused her to worry." Grace heaved a sigh. "I hate to admit that she sometimes rubs me the wrong way."

"She can be a brown-eyed Brillo pad, for sure."

Grace cleared her throat. "I knew I could count on you."

"For what?"

"To set me straight and to make me laugh through my tears."

"We make a good team. You just helped me make a decision. I was ready to throw in the towel. After talking to you, I realized it would be a selfish thing to do."

"You're a good friend. I'm so grateful for you."

Elaina's heart swelled with affection. "You cleverly diverted the question I was going to ask. Do you want me to save it for later?"

"Go ahead and ask."

Trying to be as delicate as possible, Elaina kept Dalton's name out of the inquiry. "Did Cody apply pressure?"

In a low voice Grace confirmed he had. "I'd like to say you're imagination is running amok, but I'd be lying. Damn. Hold on. Someone just cut me off."

"Where are you?"

"On Route 30."

"Do not give that person the bird"

"Too late. I already flipped him off."

Elaina felt a sense of relief. Grace would be okay. She was laughing and flipping people off. Both were good signs. Well, giving someone the bird wasn't a good thing, but it meant Grace was still in control. "Did someone really cut you off or was it another clever dodge?"

"It wasn't a dodge. Some arse passed a semi and swung into my lane too soon. I could read his license plate without squinting."

"Back to Cody. Tell me what he said."

Grace sniffed. "He said I should get me some. And no, he didn't word it differently. I'm his mother for crying out loud."

"Kids don't dance around the issues like we do. They say exactly what's on their minds. Unless it's something about them."

"I can't ground him. What were you saying about throwing in the towel?"

"Did I mention we have a cat?"

Chapter Twenty

~ Bat-crap Crazy ~

"I have fences to mend, Lula. Wish me luck."

The cat she'd impulsively named Lula, purred.

Elaina parked the Escalade in the driveway behind Grace's Equinox, noting that Tawny and Steph's cars occupied the garage. "Do you suppose they're sending me a message by taking my spot? Are they marking their territory?"

Juggling the cat carrier and three Wal-Mart bags stuffed to the max, Elaina started to the house. The moment she stepped on the grass the sprinkler system came on. Instead of being sprinkled, she was blasted. Water cascaded over her like a waterfall, drenching everything including her bra and panties.

Elaina spit and sputtered. "This is so not funny." Her gut said it was a deliberate act. It had to be. When Arden had the system installed, it had been calibrated for a gentle mist and set to come on at six o'clock in the morning, not six at night. Soaked to the gills, she adjusted the carrier and packages, and slogged to the door. "It. Is. On." If those hooligans had something to say, they should've done it with conversation not water.

Reaching for the handle of the screen door, she was surprised when it swung open.

Grace stood with her eyebrows furrowed together. "What happened to you?"

"The sprinkler went rogue or it's been sabotaged." Elaina handed the carrier to Grace. "Where are Tawny and Steph?"

"Upstairs packing."

In the hallway leading to the kitchen, Elaina dropped the plastic bags and removed her soggy sneakers.

Grace sat the carrier next to Stony's food tote without posing questions about the cat.

Lula meowed to be let free.

"Sorry, girl, not yet." Elaina yanked open the drawer holding dish towels. Grabbing a towel she blotted her face and neck. "Packing, huh?"

"Tawny's steaming mad. Steph hasn't said much but you can tell she's upset."

A rush of anger consumed Elaina. "I can't win. No matter what I say or do, they take it wrong."

"I think you pulled a scab off when you told them moving in was a mistake."

Elaina ran the towel down her legs. "That's not how I worded it." She huffed out a strong breath of frustration. "To get even with me they screwed with the sprinkler."

Grace scrunched her face in confusion. "If they did, it happened before I got here." She looked at her watch. "I've been home for almost two hours. By the way, you're not the only one on Tawny's shit list. She reamed me good when I got home."

"Oh yeah?" Tossing the towel on the counter, Elaina placed her hands on her hips. "It's time to have it out."

"Maybe you should count to ten before you go up."

"One. Two. Three. Ten." Elaina sprinted up stairs; her heart pounding with adrenaline. She stopped at Tawny's room first.

"You finally came home." Tawny heaped a stack of jeans into an open suitcase. "I'll be out of your hair in a little bit."

Grace had said they were packing but to actually see it happening was a jolt that rocked Elaina to the core. The plan to rip into her about the sprinkler fell away. "Why are you leaving?"

"You don't want us here. Frankly, I don't want to be here anymore. There's too much needless drama."

Elaina wouldn't point out that Tawny was a big contributor to the drama. She slumped onto the bed even though she was still soaked to the skin. "Where's Stony?"

"In my car."

Elaina felt the life drain out of her. Not only was she losing Tawny and Steph, but also Stony. Her heart shattered. "Where will you go?"

"Not your concern." Tawny jammed the lid closed on the overstuffed suitcase. "This was a great idea in the beginning, but like you said, it was a mistake."

"I didn't say it was a mistake. I said we didn't think things through."

"It's the same thing."

"No it isn't." Elaina blinked back tears.

Tawny plopped a second suitcase on top of the first one and emptied her lingerie drawer into it.

"Don't go."

"It's too late. My mind's made up. So is Steph's."

As if on cue, Steph stepped into the room. When she spied Elaina she ducked back out.

Elaina went after her. "Steph, wait. You're blowing this out of proportion." Where was Grace? She needed her help to convince these two lug heads to stay.

Steph put her palms up. "We tried something and it didn't work. Instead of getting in each other's way day after day, we're doing the smart thing by moving out."

Grace's head bobbed above the railing on the staircase.

"Get over here," Elaina prompted.

Grace came without being forced. She tucked her hair behind her ears. "You don't have to catch me up. I've been listening. For the record, this hasn't been a complete disaster. We had some fun."

Elaina picked up on something heart wrenching; not in Grace's words but in her tone. "Are you leaving too?"

Grace's eyes watered. "It's for the best. Living together has been," she paused, "interesting. I'm not angry with any of you, but we all have baggage that keeps haunting us and causing problems. The only true way to get our lives in order is to have our own space."

Overwrought with emotion, Elaina found herself in the kitchen. How she got there, she had no clue. Hoisting the cat carrier in her arms and snatching up the three Wal-Mart bags again, she left. This unraveling of friendship was her fault. She'd urged them to invade her space. When they did, she let little things get under her skin. A few careless words and voila! She'd hurt the three people she cared for the most. The monkeys would go their own way and the circus would soon be history.

Speeding down First Street with tears stinging her eyes, she made it to the gym without getting a ticket. It was well-past closing time, so the place was empty. She could kick, scream, swear, and lose her sanity without anyone being the wiser. Well, Lula would know but all she could do was meow.

Before going inside, she allowed Lula the freedom to stretch and take care of cat business.

It dawned on Elaina that she'd let Grace down by not having a deeper discussion about Dalton. She also owed Tawny the same consideration. They'd only scratched the surface on those conversations. Maybe Steph had been slipping out to sleep with Corbett. Anything was possible.

Once inside the gym, regret and sadness slammed into Elaina. She braced against the elliptical machine and slid to the floor with the cat in her lap. "It feels like I'm going through another divorce. This one hurts worse than the first."

* * *

"Hey, lovely lady, what's shakin'?" Michael studied her intently.

He was fishing, and for good reason. She hadn't been herself this week. Instead of being cordial to her customers and sweet to Michael, she'd erected a higher, more impenetrable fence. She wasn't letting anyone in until she was darn good and ready; or at least until she was wiser. Choosier. Unwilling to be taken in by someone else's problems. "I'm entrenched in boring computer work. The half-off membership drive I ran this week was a success. I have thirty new members."

"Excellent." Michael hem-hawed. "I ran into Grace today at the bank."

"That's nice." Elaina tried to appear unconcerned. She looked from Michael to the computer and typed in the information for a set of twins who'd joined together to keep each other motivated.

He cleared his throat to get her attention. "She said your wine club has been disbanded."

It took monumental effort to keep her expression void of emotion when her heart was doing some erratic thumping. "Things have changed."

"Are you okay with how things have changed?"

"Definitely." Non-stop fibbing was fast becoming the norm.

"Why don't I believe you?"

Elaina tapped the keyboard. "Things didn't work out. Life goes on."

"I'm sure whatever happened can be fixed."

"I don't want to talk about it, Michael."

"Okay. I'll butt out – after I say one thing. The longer you put off talking to Grace, Steph, and Tawny the harder it will be to repair the damage."

"Damage? What damage?" Elaina could feel herself becoming hysterical. Trying to power down, she apologized. "I'm sorry." She couldn't look at him for fear of falling apart.

"Let me help."

Elaina shook her head. "I made this mess. It's up to me to clean it up. Or not."

"You gals were good together. What one didn't think of, the other did. You can't let something that great fall by the wayside."

She finally met his eyes. "Think about it. Four women living together. What could possibly go wrong? Easy answer: everything."

Getting nowhere, Michael shoved his gym bag up on his shoulder. "You have my card. When you're ready to accept my help…or to get naked…give me a call." He clicked his tongue and walked away.

* * *

At the end of her shift, Elaina made a trip to the bank to deposit the days' receipts. Normally, she looked forward to heckling Grace while she worked. Today, she dreaded the occasion.

Grace greeted her with a warm smile and inclined her head to the right.

Elaina drew back at the sight of Arden. The f-word rolled off her tongue. Handling the pressure of seeing Grace was one thing. The strain of her ex was quite another. The deposit could wait until tomorrow. She turned to leave. From the corner of her eye she caught Grace giving Arden the brush by putting the 'closed - move to the next teller' sign in her window.

Arden's look of irritation was priceless.

Grace didn't stop there. She placed another sign in the next teller's window.

Elaina laughed behind her hand when she noticed the sign had a reversible arrow pointing back to Grace's window.

Arden wasn't amused. "Call her off, Elaina, or I'll complain to her boss."

Elaina rolled her eyes. "You still lack a sense of humor, Arden. Thank God Grace has one."

Grace's boss stepped from his office. He looked around like he sensed something wasn't quite right.

Elaina squinted and dared Arden to nark. To her shock, he pretended everything was exactly as it should be. When his business was concluded, he said, "Stay out of trouble, ladies."

They watched him walk away.

"Arden has left the building," Elaina announced. "And the bloodhound is back in his office."

"Before I met you, Elaina, I was afraid to act up. Now I can't stop." Grace giggled.

"That's a good thing, right?"

"It's the best." Grace's smile drooped. "I miss you, Tawny, and Steph."

The bank was suddenly crowded with customers, forcing Grace to complete Elaina's transaction.

Elaina found it difficult to walk away. "I have a bottle of white Merlot with your name on it. Stop by sometime and we'll crack it open."

* * *

"I'll have two strip steaks, two chicken breasts, and two pounds of ground turkey." Elaina gave the guy in the white uniform behind the meat counter the eye. Steph's crush.

"Coming right up."

Jack Kirby was stocky with love handles. He had a thick head of sandy-hair and deep-green eyes that smiled when he spoke. No wonder Steph found him irresistible. Elaina thought about the night when things had gone awry with Steph. Was the ice cream fiasco because of Jack? Did Steph put the moves on him only to find out he was married or already involved? God she wished she could have a do-over and take the time to find out what had been behind the anxiety. If she would've been more sensitive to the situation, whatever the situation was, maybe the four of them would still be one big, happy, dysfunctional…circus.

"I want to change my order."

"Ma'am?"

"Make that four steaks, four chicken breasts, and four pounds of ground turkey."

"Ohhh-kay."

"Add four boneless pork chops." She pointed to the meat case. "And that pork loin is going home with me as well."

Green eyes glistened with interest. "I have a feeling there's more going on here than amending your order."

"You're very wise, Jack."

He ran a hand over his chin. "That's not something a guy hears every day."

Elaina steepled her hands over her mouth and nose. "Just so you know I'm not flirting."

"No, ma'am, you're not. What *are* you doing?"

"Getting a feel for why Stephanie Mathews can't stop talking about you." *Please, God, I'm doing this for Steph. Don't let it bite me in the hiney.*

Elaina could tell the moment realization dawned. Jack's polite smile grew into something more personal.

"She can't stop talking about me?"

"Nope. It's Jack this, Jack that." Elaina used her hand to mimic Steph's chattering. "The woman never shuts up about you." She was laying it on thick, but if she was going to lie it might as well be a whopper.

He looked stunned. "I had no idea."

A flash of what-if was as good as a flick to the forehead. What if Jack *was* married? His wife might go after Steph with a ball bat. Maybe she should leave the store right now and never come back. "You're not married, are you?"

"It's a little late to be asking that question."

"Sometimes my mouth gets ahead of my brain."

"I'm not married, engaged, or currently dating."

"Whew! I was sweating there for a minute."

"Does Steph really talk about me or were you yanking my chain?"

"She does." Elaina corrected the remark. "She did. We had a falling out but I know she's still hung up on you."

Two elderly ladies wandered to the counter.

"Why are you telling me this?"

Because I want Steph to be happy. "In case you feel the same way about her but are too shy to make the first move."

Jack tapped the counter, not focusing on her or anything in particular, but Elaina knew the cogs were turning.

One of the women intruded. "Young man, can I get some Colby cheese?"

"You sure can. I just need to get a phone number from this gal, then I'll be right with you."

"Ohhh. Magic is afoot."

Elaina wrinkled her nose with happiness. "It sure is." She scribbled Steph's cell phone number on a Post-It note.

* * *

Elaina eyed the emergency room receptionist. She couldn't say she needed blood work done without paperwork to back it up, which meant, she had to fake appendicitis. Clutching her right side, she ambled up to the desk with a loud moan.

The woman looked over the top of her reading glasses. "What's going on, hon?"

A moan louder than the first was Emmy material. "I think…" Really getting into the role, Elaina bunched her face in pain. "How can you tell if your appendix is about to burst or if the pain is just gas?" Holy cow, she'd said that with a straight face.

"A doctor and possibly a blood draw will have to make the determination. Have a seat. I'll try to speed through the paperwork so we can get you looked at."

"Mmm. Ahhh."

"Name?"

"Tawny Westerfield."

"Excuse me?"

"Is Tawny here?"

"Ohhh, I thought you were saying you were her. I know Tawny, and you're not her." The woman's eyes narrowed. "I thought for a second I might have to call security."

Elaina inserted another small groan. "Tawny's my friend. She'll know what to do."

The woman's eyebrows rose as if to say 'we've got a live one'. "I'll see if I can get a hold of her. In the meantime, have a seat."

Elaina started to sit down.

"Over there." The receptionist pointed to the row of seats in the waiting room.

"Thank you." Still faking a hobble, Elaina slowly made her way to the chair closest to the sliding doors, in case the receptionist actually called security.

Keeping an eye pealed for Tawny, she was surprised when it took less than five minutes for her to show up.

Tawny spoke a few words to the receptionist before proceeding to Elaina. Dressed in a white lab coat with a pair of latex gloves hanging from the pocket, she looked every bit the nurse. Nurses were supposed to be sweet and caring. This particular nurse looked as though she wanted to jam a needle into Elaina and wiggle it around. "I hear you have a monster of a side ache."

Elaina put a hand on her left side knowing full well appendicitis would be on the right. "My appendix is misbehaving."

"Really?" There was plenty of 'you've got to be kidding' in the one-word question.

"I could barely get out of the car."

"You don't have a car. You have an SUV."

"I saw Grace earlier," Elaina blurted.

"Was this before or after you decided to put on this charade?"

"You wound me. My side hurts."

Tawny hit her with a stout blast of irritation. "I know what this is and I don't appreciate being pulled away from people who really need me."

"I need you," Elaina said under her breath but loud enough for Tawny to hear.

"You're bat-crap crazy."

Elaina straightened. "I'm trying to reach out to you, Tawny. But if you want to remain pigheaded, then fine."

Chapter Twenty-One

~ The Circus Is Back In Town ~

Tawny and Arden's assessments were correct. She was a loon; a complete and utter nut job. Her behavior over the past several weeks was proof.

Elaina wandered to the patio with the cat tucked under her arm and a mug of piping hot coffee. "Well, Lula. What do you think? Should I sell the gym and move to Texas? If I'm starting over – yet again – I should do it in Dallas where I won't trip over my ex husband or my ex friends."

Earlier in the day was the first time she'd stepped into the bedrooms once occupied by Tawny, Steph, and Grace. She'd tried not to cry but failed miserably when she found clothes and shoes still in their closets. At some point they'd show up to collect the rest of their belongings. Elaina wasn't sure she could handle them leaving all over again. The closet discovery prompted another one. None of their items had been removed from the storage building. For the briefest of moments she allowed the possibility they weren't permanently gone.

Just as quickly, she realized hanging onto hope would lead to more heartache.

Sitting in a chaise, Elaina sat the cat in her lap and scanned the extravagant back yard. There was an in-ground pool, an eight-person hot tub, a stone fire pit, trees for shade, a patio with enough space to host a large party, and of course, the man-cave storage building. She didn't need any of those things. Of course, if she relocated to the Lone Star state, she'd need a pool.

She startled Lula with a heavy sigh.

Moving away from Cherry Ridge had to happen if she was to have a chance at being happy again. Her eyes watered. "No. No. No," she said defiantly. "No more crying."

Lula meowed and snuggled deeper in her lap.

"I'm surprised you're still my friend after what I had the vet do to you." She smoothed the fur on Lula's back. "You're lucky. You can win friends and affection just by being you. I, on the other hand, lose more people than I gain by being me."

Today she'd had one of her employees take the deposit to the bank because she couldn't bear to bump into Grace. She'd put herself out there for all three members of the wine club and the effort had fallen flat.

Grace hadn't taken the hint to stop by to share the bottle of wine, or she rejected the idea. Steph didn't call to chew her out or acknowledge that she'd stuck her nose in where it didn't belong. Tawny had made it clear she'd been a nuisance.

"If I get a real appendicitis I'd be wise to find another

hospital." She snickered but her heart clenched.

Instead of drowning her sorrows in wine, she'd been drinking massive amounts of coffee hoping the caffeine intake would get her over the emotional hump. So far all it did was make her jittery.

Using her phone, Elaina searched the Internet for the most popular realtor in Cherry Ridge. Dialing Macintosh Realty, she expected to get an answering machine since it was well past five o'clock.

As luck would have it, someone picked up on the first ring. "Macintosh Realty. Jess speaking."

A blast of indecision locked Elaina's jaw. Jess Macintosh – a.k.a. Mac – was a fellow member of the Chamber of Commerce and Arden's golfing buddy. Although, it didn't matter which realty company she called, Arden was well-connected. The news she was putting her properties up for sale would be pipelined to him before she went back inside to refill her coffee mug.

"Hello," Jess said, trying to prompt a conversation.

"Mac, this is Elaina Samuels." She paused.

"Elaina! It's so good to hear from you, sweet lady! "

No overload of sugar there. "How are you, Mac?"

"Doing great. Roberta was just saying the other day that it's been ages since we've seen you."

"It's been a while."

"Sorry to hear about Arden."

That was an odd way to word their divorce since it involved her too. Oh well, it didn't matter. She didn't call for sympathy. "Thanks." Elaina opened and closed the sip tab on the insulated coffee mug. "The reason I called was to see if you'd consider listing my home and the gym. I may be moving to Dallas soon and I need a realtor who will work hard to sell both places quickly."

"I'm your man." There was an undeniable cha-ching in his voice.

Mac's statement made her think of Michael. He'd been trying to be her man since the day he introduced himself. How would he take her leaving? In the big scheme of things, she was glad they hadn't engaged in anything more than casual lust.

"Stop by sometime and we'll get the appraisals underway." Elaina didn't want to go into the fine points of the properties over the phone because taking the first step to a new life was making her nauseous. Or maybe it was the five cups of coffee she'd had since lunch.

"I'm glad you singled me out…to take care of you."

Elaina held the phone away and glared at it. There were guys known to prey on newly-divorced women. Jess Macintosh sounded like one. He was probably just buttering her up, but hell, what she knew about men would fit in a thimble. She thought she'd known everything about Arden. Ha. That low-down, shiftless… Name calling was immature and detrimental to a new beginning. It was time to forgive and forget. Arden was moving on and she needed to do the same – with a pure heart and a clear head.

"Are you still there?"

"Yes." She curbed her suspicion of Mac. He wasn't flirting. He was schmoozing. "I came to you because you're the best in the business."

Instead of humility she got the cocky side of him. "You know it."

"I've got to go. My phone's beeping with another call. Talk to you soon."

"Before you go, I wanted to thank you for giving me your business. Although I'm surprised you didn't give Arden and his fiancée first dibs. He's foaming at the mouth to get the house back. We could make him pay through the nose for it."

"His fiancée?" Elaina went numb. Not even divorced for two months and he's engaged?

"Shit. You didn't know?"

She could hear Mac bashing himself in the background for being an idiot.

"I didn't."

"I'm terribly sorry, Elaina."

"No worries, Mac. Really. I won't say a word."

"You're an awesome lady. Arden was a fool to let you go."

LET ME GO? She shouted silently. The word *let* implied he *allowed* her to leave. Arden didn't *let* or *allow* anything. He left. Elaina started to laugh, joyfully. Arden was no longer her problem. She pitied the woman he would now boss around. Since he and his fiancée were a hasty happening, they couldn't possibly know everything about each other. Elaina hoped the new Mrs. Samuels had a dark side; a really, really dark side that included whips and chains. It would serve him right to marry a dominatrix who would tie him up, clamp electrodes to his nipples, and spank him when he got out of line.

Micromanage that, Arden!

Elaina made a snap but firm decision to keep her butt in Cherry Ridge. There's no way she'd miss out on the smell of burnt nipple hair.

"Umm, Mac, I've decided to hold off on putting my properties on the market."

Mac groaned. "I screwed up. Dammit."

"No you didn't. I was on the fence anyway. You gave me a small push to the right side of the fence."

Before Mac could whine further about his mistake or make her feel guilty for losing out on some big money, she said, "My phone's beeping again. I really have to go." She hit the end button to disconnect the call.

Arden had tried to convince her she needed to self-soothe. She was going to self-sooth all right – with wine.

"Elaina!"

The shout had come from the front of the house. Elaina was out of the chaise in a nano-second. "Back here, Grace," she hollered.

Grace came into view with a hand on her chest. Her eyes and the tip of her nose were red from crying.

Alarm coursed through Elaina. "What's wrong?"

"Stony's missing!"

Every nerve in Elaina's body felt like they short-circuited. "What do you mean he's missing?"

"Tawny's been staying with her cousin on Jefferson Street. When she got home from work today, she found her cousin asleep and Stony gone. Elaina, she's freaking out!"

Elaina wanted to freak out too. Stony was the bomb

when it came to dogs. He'd won her over on day one. "Where's Tawny now?"

"Out scouring the neighborhood. She called 9-1-1. That should tell you how upset she is."

"Let me put Lula in the house and I'll help look."

"If anything happens to him…"

"Don't go there, Grace." A gorgeous dog like Stony wouldn't stand a chance in the wrong hands. They had to locate him soon or he'd be gone forever.

Arriving at the place Tawny had been staying, they were met by Steph and Carter Payne.

Elaina wanted to throw her arms around Steph but feared being pushed away. "I came as soon as I heard."

"We could use the help," Steph said stiffly.

"Hi, Carter." Elaina was filled with a lot questions regarding him, but the answers would have to wait.

"Tawny's inside," he simply said.

Had Tawny given up? If he was her dog… Stony wasn't her dog. But she loved him like he was hers. "I'll say a few words before I start looking."

Elaina, Grace, and Steph found Tawny curled up in a fetal position on the sofa.

"Tawn'," Elaina said gently.

Tawny's eyelashes fluttered before she opened her eyes. "He's gone, Elaina."

Elaina's heart broke in two at seeing her friend's soul crushed. "Just temporarily." She said a quick prayer for Tawny and for guidance in finding the canine with the biggest, bluest eyes.

"I've searched to the point of exhaustion."

"Can I get you anything? A glass of water? Or cup of tea?"

Tawny's woebegone eyes watered. "Nothing, thanks."

"Come here." Elaina pulled Tawny against her. "We'll comb every inch of town. I promise. Someone's seen him."

"I don't want to sound negative, but he might've been gone for four or five hours. The longer he's gone the less chance I have of getting him back."

Elaina pushed Tawny's hair from her face. "Stay by your phone and don't give up hope." Guiding Tawny back to the sofa, Elaina kissed the top of her head.

"I'm just going to rest for five or ten minutes, then I'll go back out," Tawny said, wiping tears away.

"Okay, guys." Elaina inhaled a breath. "I'll take the northwest quadrant of town." She crossed her fingers. "Let's bring him home."

Armed with a sandwich bag of treats and a picture of Stony on her phone, Elaina set out on foot. She knocked on doors, showed Stony's picture, and left her number in case he was spotted.

"I never realized this town had so many alleys." She snooped in backyards and garages, while calling out his name.

When she got to Northend Park, she showed Stony's picture to anyone who would look, including the wee ones. One kid who was coated with sand from playing in the sandbox said he'd seen Stony earlier over by the monkey bars and had wandered over to pet him.

Elaina's heart nearly leapt from her chest. "Are you sure?"

"He licked my face."

Stony didn't know a stranger and licking faces was his M.O. It had to be him. "Did you see which way he went?"

The kid pointed toward Route 66.

Elaina kept her fears inside. Stone-man wouldn't fare well on the busy highway. "Thank you so much." She took off running.

At Route 66, she looked in each direction. There was no sign of Stony.

If she headed north it would take her out in the country. She needed her SUV for that. She'd promised to scour the entire town, so south it was.

She updated the other searchers with a quick text message.

Reaching the corner of Fifth Street and Route 66, she had to wait for a semi tractor-trailer rig to go by. "Michael." Digging his card from her wallet, she punched in his number.

"Hello."

She didn't hear the roar of a diesel engine. "It's Elaina."

"No really. Who is it? Am I being pranked?"

"Are you trying to be funny?"

"You don't sound like the Elaina Samuels I know."

Awareness dawned. "That's because my throat is dry and scratchy. I've been hollering for Stony. He's lost, Michael. I'm out looking for him. I wondered if you wanted to help."

"Of course, I want to help. What should I do? Where should I go?"

Elaina brought him up to snuff with the search.

"Is there any chance you could recruit Dalton James?" As soon as the question was out of her mouth, she questioned the wisdom of involving Dalton without Grace's permission. Would she ever learn to butt out?

"Who's Dalton James?"

"A friend of Grace's."

"I'll see if I can locate him. I'm glad you called. I've been going nuts trying to wait you out."

"You have?"

"Yes, ma'am."

"Ma'am," she repeated and another light bulb went on. "Would you be willing to also call Jack Kirby?"

* * *

Dusk settled in, followed by the black of night. The overcast sky from earlier was still hanging around, not allowing even a sliver of moonlight to get through.

The search party had kept in contact by phone but now it was time to meet up and decide what to do next.

The apartment Tawny was temporarily staying in wasn't big enough to hold everyone.

"Let's go to my place," Elaina suggested.

Tawny balked. "What if Stony comes back?"

Carter Payne stepped up with his thoughts. "Would your cousin keep a lookout for him?"

Around ten, they arrived at Elaina's – seven cars in all.

Steph caught up with Elaina at the door. "When this is over, I'm going to chew you out for bringing Jack into this."

Elaina was too tired to get excited. "You have every right to be mad. But thanks for saving it for later."

Eight people congregated in the kitchen.

Elaina pulled two bottles of wine from the fridge. "Anyone care for a drink while we figure this out?" Her eyes dropped to the tote still stowed by the sliding doors and she silently whimpered.

The decorative lamppost on the edge of the patio beamed just enough light for her to detect movement. She smashed her nose against the glass of the door to get a get a better look. "Oh sweet Jesus! Please be him." She fumbled with the flip-lock. "Tawny, come quick."

Stony, in all his hairy glory, stood by the pool. He'd found his way…home! Elaina was beside herself with joy.

The adorable pooch yowled and ran toward them. He got to Elaina first and lunged to lick her face. She happily welcomed his slobbery kiss.

The moment he saw Tawny he dropped to his feet, wagged his tail, and yowled even louder.

Tears of joy streamed from Tawny's eyes. And from Elaina's.

Elaina stepped back to give Tawny and Stony a few special moments to reunite.

The others held off too.

Tawny finally wiped her eyes and looked at Elaina. A fast and furious hug took place.

"Thank you. Thank you. Thank you."

"No. Thank you, Tawn'. Without you I would've never known the love between a woman and her dog."

* * *

"This doesn't change a thing. The wine club is still done." Steph wouldn't meet anyone's eyes.

Elaina's throat constricted. She was astounded and hurt. Not that Stony was a fix-all, but he'd brought them back together for a few hours. She hung her head in defeat.

Michael squeezed her hand. "Guys, I think we should go so the ladies can talk."

"You're not leaving," Steph spouted like she was commander-in-chief.

Michael quirked a cautious grin. "Are you going to hold us hostage?"

"If I have to."

Elaina lifted her eyes to Michael's in silent plea.

"I have a load of car parts that say otherwise." He brought Elaina's hand to his lips. "Thanks for allowing me to be part of this happy ending. Stony, I mean."

Elaina stepped on her tip toes and brushed his lips with a kiss.

Michael drew back just enough to show his surprise. "Stony, I owe ya, bud. If you didn't run off I never would've gotten that kiss." He leaned in and lightly pecked Elaina's mouth. "I hate to go, but I know you and your friends need to hash things out."

Dalton made googley eyes at Grace but bypassed her lips with a kiss to the forehead.

Carter nudged Tawny with his shoulder. Either he wasn't comfortable with an audience or they hadn't taken things to the swapping-spit level.

And then there was Jack. He clearly didn't understand any of this. "See you soon, Steph."

She nodded.

Elaina concluded in that moment, whatever was ailing Steph was bigger than diet failure or whatever sins they'd committed.

"Let's go, guys. It's time to give the wine club some space."

Elaina whispered her thanks.

Michael winked and stumbled out the back door, with the other guys on his heels.

Straight away, Grace lit into Steph. "We're celebrating finding Stony and you're being a pain. What gives?"

"It's okay, Grace." Elaina was afraid things would get downright ugly before they got better. After the emotion-packed hunt for Stony she was spent and would just as soon save the altercation for tomorrow, or next week, or next month. Or never.

"It's not okay. We're all guilty of stepping on each other's feelings from time to time, but it doesn't warrant us moving out and it certainly doesn't call for catty behavior." Grace bent to look at Lula who'd taken refuge under the table when Stony came into the house. "I shouldn't compare your behavior to Steph's, Lula. You're a hell of a lot nicer."

Stony lay watching Lula's every move and his sense of smell was doing double time. His nose constantly twitched. The poor guy was outnumbered. Five females in one house was a bit much for any male to handle.

Tawny circled Steph with her arms. "I don't have the strength to do battle. If you have something to say, just say it. Clear the air."

"When…when I…" Steph stepped away from Tawny. Turning her back, she sauntered to the back door.

Elaina was determined to go after her if she walked out.

Tawny slid a glance to Elaina for guidance.

Elaina shook her head and put her hand up to keep Tawny where she was.

Steph ran her fingers over the metal of the door. "I'm waiting for the results of my *second* mammogram." Her voice splintered. "The first one came back as suspicious."

Elaina, Tawny, and Grace were at Steph's side before any of them took their next breath.

The 'my life sucks' remark. Shucking the diet. Pushing everyone away. It all made sense.

Elaina gave Steph's hand a gentle squeeze but she was thankful not to be the first to speak.

The nurse among them took over. "What did the first mammogram show?"

Steph closed her eyes.

"Sweetie, you don't have to wrestle this demon alone. Remember when we first met? We promised to be here for each other. It wasn't lip service. We meant it. Please, Steph, let us be here for you." Grace also closed her eyes but opened them right away.

"I have a lump."

Those three words made the world stand still for the longest moment. When the shock hit, it hit them all at the same time. In a flash, they were huddled together in what could only be described as an all-out tear fest; offering words of comfort between gulping sobs.

It took a while for the flow of tears to cease. Elaina led Steph into the family room and onto the sofa.

Tawny passed around a box of tissues. "Did the doc say when you'd get the results?"

Another round of salty emotion gathered in the corners of Steph's eyes. She blotted them but they continued to come. Pointing to her purse, she said there was a voicemail waiting on her phone. "I can't listen to it. I'm too afraid." She visibly trembled.

Elaina stretched her arms out. "Let's hold hands and say a prayer."

Bowing their heads they prayed the Our Father and Hail Mary, and asked for good news.

While they were still linked, Elaina offered her thoughts. "Draw strength from us, Steph."

"I will," she murmured. "I want to apologize for behaving so badly. It's hard to explain the emotions that exploded inside me - and the ones still detonating. I'm scared and angry. I've been going over things in my head and one thought in particular has crippled my ability to function."

Elaina's throat clogged with emotion. She felt lightheaded and scared. If anything happened to Steph she wouldn't be able to handle it.

Steph clammed up.

Tawny took her by the shoulders. "The second mammogram doesn't necessarily mean cancer. It's standard procedure if anything at all shows up. The doc needed a second look."

Elaina braved the question to draw the thing crippling Steph out in the open. "What thought in particular is wreaking havoc with you?" Expecting Steph to stall, she was surprised when she answered without wavering.

"True love has eluded me all my life. Now I may never get a chance to find it."

Elaina spoke around the baseball size knot in her throat. "You're wrong. So very wrong. True love has been knocking at your door for the last six weeks. It just isn't the form you imagined. We love you, Steph. Girlfriend love is pretty powerful stuff."

Sopping up tears with a wad of tissues, Grace seized Steph and gave her a Dutch rub. "I can't take all this bawling." Releasing her, she issued her a warm smile. "Everything Elaina says is true. We love you and I know you feel the same about us. So let's put on our big girl panties and listen to what the doc has to say. Whatever the diagnosis, we'll meet it head on. Together."

A muscle in Steph's jaw quivered. "You ladies are heaven sent and I love you with all my heart." Finding her phone, she held it out to Tawny. "Star fifteen to retrieve my voice mail."

Tawny looked from person to person and made the Sign of The Cross. She pulled up Steph's voice mail and punched in the password. Her face was lined with tension as she listened. Handing the phone back to Steph, a small smile cracked the plane of her lips and the severe lines etching her face disappeared. "It's a cyst.

A benign cyst. You don't have to undergo a biopsy or treatment. You're going to be fine."

Squeals of joy bounced off the walls. They hugged, cried more tears, and gave thanks for answered prayers.

"I'm so tired I want to sleep for days," Steph said. "But I need the lulling effect of alcohol to make it happen."

Elaina snagged four bottles of wine from the 'fridge. "White Merlot for Grace. Dry red for Tawny. Zesty Sangria for Steph. And sweet blackberry for me."

Grace smiled so big it took over her entire face. "Our own bottle like we had the day we met. The day you staged an intervention. The day we became the No Sweat Pants Allowed – Wine Club."

"Speaking of which," Elaina skirted to the closet in the hallway, "I have something for each of us." She returned with the three Wal-Mart bags she'd brought home from Port Clinton. Searching the bags, she tossed two aside. She held the third bag out to Steph.

"For me?"

"For you to distribute."

Steph peeked in the bag and a smile tugged at the corner of her mouth. "Now I'm sure I love you." She pulled out four neatly folded pairs of grey sweat pants.

"I think we should amend the name of our club to Sweat Pants Allowed – Wine Club. Life's too short and precious to sweat the small stuff but the reality is we will. We might as well do it in sweat pants."

"Amen to that." Tawny popped the corks on the wine bottles.

Grace collected four fancy glasses from the cupboard.

Steph poured.

Elaina gave the first toast. "To the unbreakable bonds of friendship and love. May they grow stronger every day."

Grace added her thoughts. "To Dalton, Carter, Jack, and Michael who probably think we're four wackos they need to steer clear of. Let's prove them wrong." She quickly added, "I'm not ready to dive into a full-on relationship but I'm ready to date."

"I agree. We need to proceed slowly," Tawny chirped.

"Same for me," Steph said. "I don't want to fall for someone who will walk all over me. I sense Jack is different, but I'm going to take my time to find out. He may not even consider me after I showed my nasty temperament."

Elaina grinned. "He's interested, Steph. Trust me."

"You and I still need to talk."

"Uh huh. We do."

"Some other time, okay?"

"Fine by me."

Clinking their glasses, Steph downed a sip of Sangria and held up her glass again. "To Elaina who brought us together."

"I played a tiny part. The big guy up stairs put us in the jewelry store. The rest was up to us."

Grace toyed with the rings she'd moved to her right hand. "I still have these."

"Some day when the time is right we'll partake in another cash-for-gold event."

"This time I won't bawl. I promise."

Elaina kissed Grace's temple. "Don't promise. If you want to cry, do it. I might even cry. Chances are I won't. Did I mention Arden's engaged?"

Steph, Tawny, and Grace's eyes doubled in size.

Steph suggested a get-even strategy.

"Only if Grace wears the catwoman mask."

They broke into a laugh.

Elaina's heart was happy. The girls were back. Stony was back. Lula had joined the motley crew. Life couldn't be better. *This **is** my circus and you **are** my monkeys.*

~ The End ~

Stay tuned for more from:
Elaina Samuels, Tawny Westerfield, Stephanie
Mathews and Grace Cordray

(Sequel coming in the fall of 2015)

About the Author

Jan Romes grew up in northwest Ohio in the midst of eight zany siblings. Married to her high school sweetheart for more years than seems possible, she's also a mom, mother-in-law, and grandmother. Jan writes contemporary romance and women's fiction with sharp, witty characters who give as good as they get. When she's not writing, you can find Jan with her nose buried in a book or finding ways to stay fit. She loves spending time with family and friends. A hopeless romantic, she finds joy in sunsets and sappy movies. Though she doesn't have a green thumb, she takes pride in growing pumpkins, sunflowers, and veggies.

You can follow Jan here:

www.authorjanromes.com
www.jantheromancewriter.blogspot.com
www.twitter.com/JanRomes
www.facebook.com/jan.romes5
www.goodreads.com/author/show/5240156.Jan_Romes

<u>Other books by Jan Romes</u>:

Texas Boys Falling Fast series
Book #1 – Married to Maggie
Book #2 – Keeping Kylee
Book #3 – Taming Tori
Book #4 – Not Without Nancy (coming soon)

One Small Fib
Lucky Ducks
Kiss Me
The Gift of Gray
Stay Close, Novac!
Stella in Stilettos
Three Wise Men
The Christmas Contract
Mr. August
Three Days with Molly
Big on Christmas

41265275R00146

Made in the USA
Lexington, KY
06 May 2015